ALSO BY JOHN CANAVAN

FocuStrategy:
Navigating Your Professioinal Growth

www.focustrategy.com

Twitter – Johncanavan@focustrategy

www.InterimGM.com

F**OCU**Strategy

Vol. II: Navigating Your Office and Leadership Challenges

▶▶▶▶

John Canavan

BALBOA.
PRESS

A DIVISION OF HAY HOUSE

Balboa Press books may be ordered through booksellers or by contacting:

Balboa Press
A Division of Hay House
1663 Liberty Drive
Bloomington, IN 47403
www.balboapress.com
1 (877) 407-4847

Because of the dynamic nature of the Internet, any web addresses or
links contained in this book may have changed since publication and
may no longer be valid. The views expressed in this work are solely those
of the author and do not necessarily reflect the views of the publisher,
and the publisher hereby disclaims any responsibility for them.

The author of this book does not dispense medical advice or prescribe the use
of any technique as a form of treatment for physical, emotional, or medical
problems without the advice of a physician, either directly or indirectly. The
intent of the author is only to offer information of a general nature to help
you in your quest for emotional and spiritual well-being. In the event you use
any of the information in this book for yourself, which is your constitutional
right, the author and the publisher assume no responsibility for your actions.

Any people depicted in stock imagery provided by Thinkstock are
models, and such images are being used for illustrative purposes only.
Certain stock imagery © Thinkstock.

Printed in the United States of America.

ISBN: 978-1-4525-1567-0 (sc)
ISBN: 978-1-4525-1566-3 (hc)
ISBN: 978-1-4525-1565-6 (e)

Library of Congress Control Number: 2014909855

Balboa Press rev. date: 06/26/2014

Acknowledgments

To my brother Michael, for his encouragement
and help throughout the process.

To my brother-in-law Shawn
who is always supportive of my efforts.

Contents

Introduction

As with FocuStrategy volume I, the writings in this book are not designed to give you detailed answers to your day-to-day challenges, but instead are a guide to build your awareness in your work environment and with those challenges. As a subordinate and/or a leader your understanding and behavior play an important role in your growth potential and fulfillment. The competitiveness, politics, unfairness and dysfunctional management that's out there requires you to be on your toes constantly and deliberately. There is always someone else vying for your position or the next promotion. Colleagues, co-workers and especially bosses are always judging and assessing - your behavior, your decisions, your likability, your work ethic, etc. Balancing all of this and understanding what to do and how to proceed on issues from what the numbers mean to the effects of the office gossiper is critical to your ambitions and professional growth. Navigating Your Office and Leadership Challenges will give you some perspective.

1

Speaking at your Meetings

When attending meetings have you noticed that they all have a specific tone? The leader of the meeting or the Inviter sets the tone and creates the justification for content and length.

- Before entering a meeting know what you're going to say, but be ready to change it in case the agenda shifts. This entails preparation. When you are not prepared, it is uncomfortable and shows.
- If a meetings tone is dull and redundant to previous meetings, look to bring new content that may drive and open up discussion. At a minimum you break up the dead air and you look progressive.
- Make sure you have your key points laid out in a way that you can flow from one-to-another. There is nothing more confusing than bouncing from topic-to-topic. Also you will look like you're unable to hold a thought.

It's also a good habit to arrive early to meetings. It gives you an opportunity to speak with others before the meeting begins and can give you some insight as to what other topics will be brought up. The points you bring up in meetings should be concise and substantive. Speak with confidence and authority on the points you bring.

2

When you Fail

The reaction is different for everyone when they fail. Some shut down, others blame others, and some accept defeat and move on. When you manage a team/department your reaction is important to the morale and disposition of the people you manage as they learn from you. A few things to consider.

- Regardless of fault do not blame others. The temptation is there especially when it's blatantly obvious. You can show your annoyance, but move on quickly. Looking at variables and assessing why and how is helpful and will give you insight as to cause.
- Think. Avoid reacting impulsively. In more cases than not you will more than likely exasperate the issue. Talk to other involved (not allowing them to blame) and work through the issue. Make sure your intentions and directions are clear so you don't fail twice on a similar issue.

- Avoid thinking that you are the smartest in the room. Don't make assumptions about others on your team/ department. They may have made decisions based on poor information they received or direction.

The bottom line is that people's intentions (mostly) are good and when there is a failure they are feeling just as bad as you are. The way you deal with it is the way they will deal with it. Shut down and sulk and your next project will not go so well. Blame others and you have justification and an outlet to fail again. Accept blame and move quickly to adjust and deal with the issue head-on.

3

Nice Job

Regardless of how high or low you are on the totem-pole it's good to hear, "Nice job." We all have our good days and bad days. It's not easy to be on-point all the time. As a manager your job is to support the performance and growth of your subordinates. It does not take a lot to explain and jolt someone into a certain direction.

- Being critical of your subordinates less than stellar performance and/or constantly pointing out errors does not do anyone any good. It shows your lack of leadership, reduces the morale of your subordinate and they will work just that much less, and it is bad for productivity.
- Letting subordinates know that their work is pertinent and worthy goes a long way in upping their morale and performance. When they feel a part of something they contribute with self-worth.

- As a leader it is your responsibility to increase your subordinate's performance. Moving beyond your critical thoughts of someone its good habit to show them you're not petty and concentrated on their missteps.

Your subordinates know when you're unhappy about something and it sets the tone for their day. This is not to say that will not have any performance HR issues with subordinates, but it is your job to build on the strengths, not weaknesses. Finding those strengths is leadership. Telling someone, "Nice job" does not put you in a box when praising a specific job.

4

Prioritize

Being able to prioritize is essential for accuracy, productivity, performance, results and ROI. When you are chasing too many priorities it is detrimental to an overall plan (if there is one) and the most significant problem is distraction and chaos. Not only are you all over the place, but your subordinates and colleagues are as well.

- Wherever the directives are coming from you need to be able to articulate your concern about the conflicting prospects of prioritizing too much. As a leader it is your responsibility to shape direction.
- Don't be afraid to have a routine. Routines allow you to prioritize efficiently. Without that predictability your outcomes are unpredictable, hence constant adjusting.
- Focus and delegate. When you stay focused on pertinent priorities the process of working through those priorities is less confused and more accurate.

Being able to delegate the peripheral priorities allows for the same.

Everything is a priority today and your initiative in managing those priorities is imperative to the efficiency of the process. You must know what priorities will have the return the organization is looking for within the context of its mission and goals.

5

What is Coming

Your boss and your company rely on you more than you know to let them know what is coming...what technologies are next, what will give your company a competitive advantage, etc. It is very frustrating being a leadership and watching your competitors go by and not receiving innovational or creative ideas from your staff. You need to be aware of what is coming by putting yourself out there.

- Although consulting firms have value, the consulting should be just part of what you accept as a source of information. Listen, but seek out yourself.
- Go to tech shows, (even on your own dime) as the people you meet there and the demonstrations will give you more insight as to what is hot and what may-be not.
- Speak to grade school students, high school students, college students, your kids, their kids, etc. Understanding their interests will put you in a unique

position... they usually know what is coming before most.

Technological trends are tricky because you cannot know what is a fad or what will stick and grow. But, at a minimum, exposing yourself to areas where new technologies begin... puts you ahead of most and will give you that much more advantage when asked for new ideas.

6

A Good Manager

...Leads by knowing what their subordinate's needs are. Telling them what they need instead of asking them what they need is a sure way of sending a project or their career off the rails.

- Sometimes you will ask your managers or staff what they need... and they honestly may not know, or they are afraid to ask. It's your responsibility to put them at ease and figure out what will help.
- Be prepared for complaints about their colleagues, about your performance, and perhaps some things that you do not want to hear about. But, that comes with it. You need to navigate this and place them back on track in a way that makes them feel supported, or at least listened to.
- Looking at things from the outside does not always give you the best perspective. Listen for what they are

not saying and do what you can to create a productive environment.

There are all kinds of people, and being able to lead all kinds of people is a talent. This talent can be learned and is a powerful tool in your success. Knowing what the needs are of people that answer to you is critical to your success and their success. Why put anyone at a disadvantage if you don't have to, especially when all you have to do is ask a question.

7

Analyzing

We have all heard the expression, don't over analyze. Well, that may true as it can waste time and bring up issues that are more confusing than not, but analyzing in an effort to help your company stand out from the pack is more than required. Analyzing takes time, effort, intelligence, patience and evaluating. It's not easy when done properly and thoroughly. But, without it you are simply flying by the seat of your pants or following a competitor.

- By setting up an analytical process you slowly bring an understanding and strategy for advantage. Knowing who your customers are and what they want/need is critical to separating yourself out from the pack.
- Analyzing properly, (and this means investing in software and people) allows you to disseminate information to the point of details that make a difference to customers, employees and the market in general.

- When everyone on your team understands and supports what value analyzing brings, it will create an innovative process that impacts costs, behavior, interest, creativity and attention to trends taking place – which quite frankly are always.

Analyzing data can seem a real chore, especially if you don't see the results of the implemented process based on what has been analyzed. But, again, done properly, deliberately with purpose it will be obvious when competitors look to emulate.

8

Using the Word "Team"

The definition of team is; a group that comes together to achieve a common goal. It sounds nice and the word is used a lot, but its meaning in many aspects has lost its true value within organizations.

- A team shares a common goal and strategy. A team holds criticisms back of other members as the words team and criticism contradict each other.
- The team leader includes all on the team of strategy and keeps inclusive communication streaming in order to avoid miscommunication and devaluing.
- Identifying the strengths of each team player so their talents can be honed and coordinated with others on the team is beyond required for you and your team to be successful.

If you are responsible for a group of people (including the full organization) and things are in disarray and/or in unfocused tension, then you are applying the word and actions of the meaning wrong. Everyone needs to be comfortable on the team so they can contribute to its goal and purpose comfortably and confidently. Otherwise it is not a team, it's just a bunch of people going to work.

9

If Your Team is Not Working

Then you have some adjusting to do. Sometimes the team you have in place just does not mesh right. It can be a combination of things...personality conflicts, poor leadership, talent gap, or maybe the strategy is off. Whatever it may be adjustments need to be done.

- Putting people together that are mature enough to argue a point and not offend or be offended by a push back is important because it lessens the chance of hurt feelings and less openness.
- Too many people on a team confuses issues. People forget what was said and who said what and challenges keep recycling bringing you no closer to the objective.
- A strong and fair leader is pertinent to the success of a team's performance. Someone unbiased and balanced in their views.

The problem with teams (or having so many competing views in one room) is that everyone is vying for position and notoriety. That is why it is so important to manage a team in a way that promotes cohesion and attention to each member. When people on the team are not afraid of losing their job or being chastised for an unusable idea they will flourish in a cooperative and valued way. However, sometimes a member or two just are not conducive to the team and may be a weak link... switching them out may be necessary. It happens.

10

Stuff Happens

You have a plan…everything is going according to plan, then all of a sudden your plan is off the rails. Well, first of all you should have known something like this could happen. Second of all, what will you do now?

- Think. You need to calm yourself down, avoid panicking or being impulsive and think through the challenge.
- Wishing and hoping are just that, wishing and hoping. That won't get you back on track. You need to assess your situation, contemplate the effects of slowing, going forward or changing direction completely. But, in a calm manner. When your adrenaline is pumping you need to dilute it so you don't go 90 miles an hour in a bad direction/decision.
- Once you have decided a course of action, deal with it. Just because the plan went off the rails does not

mean the goal or objective is unobtainable. Adjust your course and move on.

Being cognoscente/aware of your situation and monitoring your actions going forward will help in alleviating the stress that comes with an unexpected (that you should have expected something) change of plans. It gives you a sense of being back in control... albeit, only a sense.

11

Talent

Retaining talent is a major responsibility of management and it should be listed as one of the top priorities in any organization. Providing employees with growth potential, inclusive challenges and a positive environment to pursue the goals of the organization is a sure way of retaining the right people and keeping morale high. Engaging your employees to consider what is in front of them engages their interest, hence morale. Allowing your staff to demonstrate their potential in turn allows them to prove their worth and gain experience. Your team, your staff, your employees, whatever... needs to be encouraged by you as a leader and the environment free of fear because fear immobilizes and suppresses talent. Retain by:

- Challenging your talent demonstrating to them that you care. That their interests are your interests, that their success is your success. Challenge their skills so they sharpen them.

- Treat your employees like you know what they are capable of. This needs to trickle down from the top... your management team must be able to identify talent and direct that talent where and when needed. Knowing their strengths (and weaknesses) allows you to properly manage their talent and provides for positive deliberate productivity. Less down time. It is the engagement of their capabilities which is key.
- Scare them and watch their flight. Organizations with a culture of fear are organizations that lose talent. Putting fear into employees, either managers or line employees, will only motivate so much. Organizations that do not take the time to prioritize talent risk losing the key drivers of an organizations success. A command and control, divide and conquer, aloof or disengagement of one or another manger/employee will simply instill a, "is it 5pm yet?" mentality.

Talent has to be one of the most wasted resources. When you are able to communicate with the people that work for you in a way that encourages their growth and sends them home feeling as if they've accomplished something...fulfilled and not afraid that they made a mistake or that their jobs are always on the line, then you will see what they aspire to, how productivity increases, how the bottom-line increases, how they give back what they receive and appreciate.

12

Politics is Everywhere

Very few of us can avoid office politics. Anytime a group of people are involved in something, law-and-behold someone is looking for an advantage. What do you do about it?

- First thing is try to stay clear. If this is not possible then manage it to your best advantage by understanding the players and what their interest or motivation are.
- As you watch the politics develop navigate your way in a way that makes it possible to get your work done without falling into a trap.
- Avoid allowing yourself to be duped or encouraged to make a statement detrimental to the organization or another (especially about your boss).

Office politics comes from people vying for position, power struggles, being disgruntled, jealous, fear, anger, you name it… wherever it is coming from and why you should at least be aware of so you can manage your way through or around it.

13

Focus on your Strengths

Usually when you are good at something you enjoy doing it. When you enjoy doing it chances are you are good at it. If you are not good at something what's the necessity in trying to get good at it? If you don't like crunching numbers, why would you expend energy and misplace your talent trying to get better at it? Look, it is good to learn new things and continuously learn, but the track to success is faster when you are good at something and you build on it.

It's a pain to work on weaknesses: Who wants to spend energy trying to move from slightly below average to slightly above? Try focusing on your strengths instead. Make what you're already good at an even greater asset. After all, if you really want to make a difference at your company, it's your strengths that will lead the way. Of course, it's more challenging to move from well above average to even more above average, but you'll enjoy it more since your strengths are things you likely already take pleasure in doing. And don't worry about having too much of a good thing. Have you ever worked with a leader who possessed too much character or was too strategic? Probably not.

14

Staying Late at Work

Sometimes it is necessary, most of the time not. A company's culture may imply that you need to work harder and stay late. That's a tough culture to be a part of, but there are alternatives, things you should consider.

- First, why? When during the day do you decide that you will stay late, or is it decided the day before or the day before that? What are you doing or not doing that is dictating these extra hours to you? Is it you, are you moving to slow or maybe you are inefficient? Perhaps your time management skills are off? Think about it.
- Circumstances do come up that require you to stay late sometimes, but it should not be a common thing. If the culture of the organization you are working for fears this into you or has created an environment where it is expected...then you need to assess who you work for. Putting in 10, 12, 14 hours a day at work is nothing to brag about – especially if you

are not reaping the benefits of high compensation, appreciation, or promotions (plural).

- Delegating work is important... it makes you more efficient and allows you to concentrate and move forward in the areas of work that require your attention more deeply. However, it is not just delegating...it is prioritizing, time management, dismissing nonsense, controlling your environment and schedule, etc.

Staying late at work is not a sin. But, if you are doing it most of the week (and perhaps on weekends) there is something wrong. Go home!

15

How the Boss Views Your Performance

Sometimes your boss will comment on their pleasure or displeasure with your performance. Many times they don't and simply rely, tolerate, accept, work with how you perform. So, there is that possibility that you don't know how your boss views your performance. With that understanding it is best to there are a few things you should do.

- Bosses dislike mean-spiritedness, vengeful behavior, unhealthy differences, etc. Healthy competition is much easier to manage and can be outright creative. Stay clear of confrontations that your boss may perceive as tedious and immature.
- Speak out and make yourself known. This does not mean blurt out anything that comes to your head. Make sure you think through issues and challenges that come up and be a part of the solution. Be selective in picking your tasks or projects taking opportunities

as they come up. It shows the boss you are not afraid of responsibility and you are assertive.

- Keep yourself up-to-date on industry happenings. Old news is no news...being current on events shows that you take an interest. If you take an interest you are better versed on facts and strategic thinking.

Conflicts result in delays and your boss who has a boss has little tolerance for looking bad due to tugs of war. Bosses identify with staff that show stability and capability. They view your performance in a wide array and will seek you opinion, advice and counsel if they have that trust. That trust will be obvious when raises and/or promotions are discussed.

16

Job Anxiety

When you are leaving for work, is that really where you want to be going? Like many people, probably not. However, many times it-is-what-it-is either through necessity, lack of a certain skill set, caught in a rut, etc. You need to do a few things differently.

- Foremost, make sure you do not bring that attitude to work. It simply does no one any good, especially yourself. To be a complaining unmotivated boss or colleague saps everyone's energy. One bad apple... you know the saying.
- If you cannot be in a job you love, love the job you have. You have to look at the positives in what you are doing – whatever they may be... it is either providing a service or product to someone. If you look at your job in those terms (albeit it will take some practice) you should be able to mentality overcome your anxieties in getting there.

- Keep yourself occupied and busy outside the office/ work. It is not a bad thing to be excited the weekend is coming. This way you are able to break things up in a way that promote a healthier mental attitude.

Ultimately it may be a matter of you doing some reflecting about yourself and figuring out where you want to be. Having job anxiety, whether it's not the field you like, your boss, changes, your performance, the location, the lack opportunities...whatever it may be, you need to figure out where you want to be, plan and work through obstacles to get there. Many times it's simply what you are or not doing. Maybe you're not challenged or fulfilled. Having job anxiety is not a good place to be for both your mental and physical health. It should be changed, but again, in the interim, try not to bring any negativism to work – it's tough on everyone that way.

17

Cohesion

The importance of cohesion in the work place (especially amongst management) is critical for a team mindset that needs to be strengthened continuously. There are three points that should be adhered to in this regard. 1) Being part of a management team regardless of revenue generated and employee counts – you represent a thin line. 2) Always be prepared for change...it will be coming. 3) Avoid petty distractions.

What's most important about what you experience in your current position, is for you to understand that it is not unique. Speaking constantly with peers, colleagues, friends, family, etc., they all have stories from where they work that would ground you in your thoughts of, "This place you work in is different and has unique issues." Not true. That said, you do have your challenges and those challenges should be handled in a way that is unique to your experiences and your organization's culture. Within your organization and your position the cohesion that management has makes the difference between dog-eat-dog and seamless productivity. Which would you want to be a part of? How do I mean?

- Understand the importance of your responsibility to the organization and what it means to your customers and the employees that answer to you. You need this awareness, and within that realm you must work very closely with your colleagues – your team. This should not be just a "job" for you. You have a great responsibility and obligation of both financial interest and human interest to your organization. Your cohesion, trust, understanding and loyalty to your colleagues in management/team and is imperative.

- Change comes…it's inevitable. You must have some idea of what changes may come about. Do not be afraid. Apply the cohesion (that I refer to above) and do not deviate. Politics and jarring for position in any organization is as normal as the tides of the Earth. There is zero you can do to change that. But, if there is something not working right or a mistake is made, DO NOT tattle, undermine or scorn - work with your Team and deal with/address whatever challenge/problem exists without having to prove/gloat to others (including your boss). Why do/would others have to know your efforts in the first place? Because you are vying for recognition or a different position? I would hope not. (Read, The Six Mistakes of Mankind). People that make mistakes themselves, many times in an effort to conceal those mistakes, shine the light on others – don't do it. As a team and cohesive unit you are obligated to focus your actions/efforts on dealing with challenges and moving forward. A blame game creates dissension and distrust. The protection of one's direct "staff" is immature and allows for error justifications. You are not the center of the universe, (despite what Sesame Street and Mr. Rogers taught you) you are part of something that shares an objective – as a team.

- Changes... You are being watched for your discipline in managing, your experience in business, your commitment to your responsibilities. By not taking it serious... the organization and you suffer. The vision for the organization becomes undermined.

- Petty distractions are the killers of discipline. It conjures up an un-seriousness that upper management sees, line employees see, that customers see, that vendors see, etc., and use these distractions to breakup an internal process that seems susceptible and vulnerable to outside interference or bad advice, hence, insulting your knowledge and experience. The idea here is not to discourage the contribution of intelligent and genuine advice/ideas/discussions from others, but politics and the "notice me syndrome" are abound, and your responsibility is to keep yourself and your department/division/organization awake and in check, stay true to your management colleagues/team and the organization's mission. Do not allow yourself to be drawn into unserious discussions, gossip, or any other petty distraction that fog your responsibility. (Don't take this the wrong way... Have fun at work, levity is good for stress, it's important that you like where you work, but have fun in a serious way.)

Remember, *"If you do not discipline yourself, someone else will."* Do you understand what this means? It means that whatever areas of yourself you do not concentrate on, and if you allow your decisions and performance to go unchecked or your direction to be altered... someone else will discipline the direction for you... many times without you even knowing what has happened. Not because others are doing things in a deviant way, but simply because the gap or void is there... others fill it because it can or needs to be filled, hence, leaving you behind and making you look undisciplined and/ or indecisive.

No gaps in cohesion...do not seek buffers. Speak to your colleagues in management directly and keep the cohesion intact.

18

External Influences

Beware of external influences within your organization or department and remember the control and loyalty needed to keep a project moving and more importantly the integrity of the organization intact.

It is imperative that the consolidation and chain of command/ directives/instruction/RFI's/questions, etc. remain intact in order to avoid dissension, confusion of direction, misunderstandings, miscommunication, etc. Any outside entities (influences) giving directives/ instructions/requests/ questions, etc. to your management team (or line employee) must be dealt with swiftly and directly. In other words, make clear to your management/project team that there is no authority and/or encouragement to involve or accept any off policy or off procedural direction with any outside entity.

Business is a serious matter. The integrity of your organization must be preserved. External influences are always present for either benefit to an external entity or to an interest outside the scope of the business's management - hierarchy. Larger businesses have more layers and stronger policies in place to deal with external influences, but, small businesses are more vulnerable to these influences.

19

Managers, Keep it to Yourself

Know your colleagues - in your office and without. They represent and reflect you. Managers represent a small percentage of the total workforce and are your network.

Managers are, YOU. Every one of them. You all have a responsibility to each other. Your shared responsibility and obligation as management is to support and learn from each other. When a manager does something or says something... it's as if you all have done or said something, regardless whether it's outside or inside the organization or department you manage. MANAGE – please look up the word in the dictionary. It's an important responsibility.

The organizations and/or departments that you are given the privilege and trust to manage, is just that, privilege and trust – if you don't understand this, you should leave the organization. The line employees within the organization/ department that you manage are not your support mechanism to badmouth other managers, again, YOU are part of something, MANAGEMENT. MANAGEMENT is a department in itself. That's where your allegiance and loyalty should be – always.

When you or your organization/department has a problem (a challenge) do not blame, criticize, badmouth, or complain about another manager in front of line employees especially. It creates dissension and not only undermines your colleagues, it undermines the vision and direction of an organization and allows for a culture of dissent and ultimately the result is not good all around. You need to put this together in your head – your mindset. YOU are not part of a gang that's called a company or department. You are part of something that is called management and you need to understand and take that responsibility very seriously.

Support, respect and deal with each other in a mature, responsible and direct way... not through line employee surrogates or other managers. You are together. Stay together.

20

Working with an Enemy

Unless you have a very strong constitution... it's not easy working with someone that's your enemy. Enemies exist for a number of reasons. Sometimes it's just a personality clash that quite frankly can be dealt with fairly easily – just stay out of each other's way or understand your professional behavior is important here. But, sometimes it's a competitive thing... vying for position or relevancy. Or, sometimes it's out right deliberate mean spirited sabotage, gossip, hate... whatever. Unfortunately it is uncomfortable, undermining and unproductive. Dealing with it becomes an effort in itself.

- Align yourself with someone that sees things your way, but that has a better relationship with that person (your enemy). They may be able to temper the hostility as a go between.
- Don't over extend yourself or capitulate to this person (your enemy) as it may just embolden their contentious stance towards you.

- Remove yourself from their sights and focus on your job only. The less you converse, respond, defend and confront your enemy, the better. When you take care of your own business and dismiss your enemy's efforts people around (including your boss) will see the truth in what's happening.

It can be downright demoralizing to have to come to work and battle someone every day. Just do your job as best you can...concentrate on your responsibilities and your bosses expectations. It may take some time, but your enemy will go away.

21

Drop it

No one likes to abandon a project they've been working on, but sometimes you have to cut your losses and move on. Dropping it does not imply failure as long as the reasons are legitimate.

- If you have started a project or policy/procedural change and a constant persistence is needed due to constant resistance... well, that may be a signal that you need to drop it and move on quickly. This is not to say that everything you do/try should come easy, but you should be able to tell if there is something unreasonable enough and warrants not going forward.
- If you are working on something that is having a detrimental effect (unanticipated) in other areas of the business, drop it quickly – at a minimum to re-assess if necessary.
- If you see that unintended negative consequences are impeding the growth or success of your project, etc.

and/or market conditions have changed and brought new light to your thinking...then drop it quickly as you do not want to have matters turn worse due to stubbornness.

- If you have a number of projects, ideas, etc. moving forward and you are unable to put the required attention I certain areas, then prioritize and drop it – come back to it later when you can prioritize.

Ideas and products are tested all of the time...just to have them fail in the market place or within your organization. The key is to be confident and smart enough to pull the plug and move on. There's no shame or failure in that... the contrary.

22

Take Advice

Everyone loves to give it... They can't get their own careers going or into shape, but they will certainly get yours into shape. Look, people's intentions are not bad, it's just the advice they give is not pertinent to your needs and is based on their personal experiences, views, perceptions and context of themselves. Taking/accepting advice (especially acting on it) should be considered only when you trust that the person giving it has your interests in mind along with experience, expertise and some wisdom in similar circumstances. Otherwise you are in for some wasted time and directional adjustments later.

- Manage the information coming to you. Listen, but be selective and cognoscente of its deliverer and why it's coming to you.
- Do not vent or complain to just anyone about your situation. A sure way to get bad advice is to not be

selective from whom you are getting it from in the first place.

- Think before you speak/ask. What is your goal? Why are you seeking advice? Advice will come back to you properly if you ask the right questions. What are the right questions? Well, you need to determine that in a honest way.

- It is NLP...you need to focus the advice on your needs. Control the conversation/advice so it does not go in all sorts of directions. The advice then becomes a complain-fest or talk about myself-fest. That doesn't help anybody.

The advice you accept is important because it will do one of three things; 1) It will set you on the wrong path. 2) It will stump/stop your path. 3) It will set you on the right path. This is why you need to consider who you are asking, why you are asking them, and most importantly what you are expecting back. You need to disseminate the information unbiasedly. Otherwise it's like doing a google search twisting the questions for the answer you want.

23

Reviews and Training

You cannot do a manager/line employee review directly after (example; a month or so) some specific training is done, especially if it's implied training or something the employee should already be trained for and/or the hiring process had screened for during that process. The employees performance, hence review then becomes a skewed review. In other words, doing an employee review right after specific training gives the employee an opportunity to say, "It's an unfair review because I was just trained." Reviews should be based on criteria and performance of the past quarter or past year.

There are points from previous review(s) that the reviewer should have worked on prior. Reviewers have some responsibility and obligation of performance, goals and objectives outside direct training. Imagine if every company did this... had training of what they should already know, then review them on it. Basic knowledge or performance that should already exist cannot be part of a review that an employee was just trained on. There's a difference between internal training for the purposes of culture, etc, and quite different training on how to manage and/or perform.

Honestly, people should feel offended having to do redundant training or implied experience training, then be reviewed on it. There is a cost to it – of something they should already know. An organization cannot give both... an advantage by training in something that an employee should already know... then give a cupcake review.

24

Being Assertive

Do you know people that are assertive? They are the pushy ones that others don't care for so much. Honestly, they get things done. There are two types of assertive people... the ones that make it a point to be in your face (not aggressively, but there) and the ones that are more diplomatic. Either way being assertive has its benefits when you manage it correctly.

- Being assertive in a way that does not repel others can benefit you by opening up other areas of interest and gaining knowledge. Your assertiveness allows you to get questions answered and allows you to move quickly through issues.
- Being assertive is perceived by others as having confidence. That confidence can help drive points and influence direction.
- Being assertive allows you to bulldoze your way through issues when, hence, again influencing the direction – influencing changes.

- Being assertive gives you presence when handled correctly and with poise.

There's no contradiction here... assertiveness to the point of rudeness simply makes you look, rude. Assertiveness when getting your points across and moving forward may not be liked by others, but certainly you won't be disliked or avoided – which can undermine your efforts.

25

The Credible Boss

To be credible to your subordinates they have to know that you understand their small picture and the organizations big picture. Many times your managers and/or line employees will not understand the big picture, which then becomes your responsibility to have them understand. It won't work all the time, especially when something seems contrary to their efforts, but at least you've tried. Some credibility efforts,

- Your subordinates need to believe and trust your direction. Getting them to do their jobs efficiently is predicated on them knowing you know how to do yours.
- Attempting to affect their performance through intimidation is silly and unnecessary. Scaring your managers and employees does not make you credible, however, it makes you incredibly ineffective. Lead through cooperation and understanding, reason. Not through intimidation, threats and tension.

- Influence and authority should be used as a credible force to get things done. Delegating in a way that helps others in their positions. Using your influence and authority to boss people around because you can does not make you a credible boss.

Understanding the processes within your organization and communicating in a way that empowers those under your direction allows you credibility. Lose that or never having it will have you struggling forward.

26

Accepting a Bad Job

It happens for many reasons. In this economy (or any economy for that matter) there are those that would say you are crazy for turning down a job offer. Quite honestly, if you're unemployed and running out of money or worse... you may have to take anything that's offered. But, consider something, consider your future and what comes after you accept a bad job or one that is not really right for you.

- You get stuck. You've got the job, the money starts rolling in (or dripping in) you've got to make the best of it, you get used to it. Then, you're stuck with it. Your career is sidetracked, perhaps for good. You need to be very careful about this. It takes constant attention and deliberate managing of your career to move ahead.
- Your performance suffers. You've heard it a thousand times... do something you don't like and you will not give it 100%. Nothing like getting stuck in the first place, then making it worse by non-performance.

- Lost opportunities. Although you may still search out opportunities that you are right for, or that are more your passion, you have to consider the distraction and time lost.

Look, it's easy for anyone that's employed (especially someone in their right field) to pretend that it's easy... and all you have to do is follow your dreams and all that. But, we know that's not really the case. The point here is to be very careful what and when you choose. Understand the consequences of your choice and constantly assess your position.

27

A Colleague, a Subordinate - Complaining or Venting

Right out of the gate...let's agree that everyone does this. It's human nature – we do this because we are attempting to work through and clear our minds of something that we are in conflict with. Everyone handles/does this in their own way. However, some rules should apply.

- Know the difference between complaining and venting. Complaining is whining about something that you have little control over or are incapable of working out a solution. Venting is a process of working through an issue and seeking a solution to it. In essence you are relieving the pressures within to deal with it in a reasonable manner.
- Be aware to whom you are complaining or venting to. Especially if you're confusing the two. If you're speaking with your boss and s/he thinks your complaining... well, you can probably kiss that promotion goodbye

and be prepared to not be taken seriously. Your boss will literally think you are incapable of handling anymore responsibility. The same can be said of a colleague... come off as a complainer and one of two things will happen, either that person will jump on the band wagon (because complainers need company) or they will use your complaining against you in the form of gossip or judging.

- Know what you are thinking. Understand the difference between the two – complaining and venting. When you understand the difference and when you know who you are speaking to, then, you can establish a point to your venting and control the context of its delivery so it actually helps you.

Again, we all do it, just be aware of how you are perceived by others. Complaints have a place when they are legitimate, venting also has a place. Try not to target others in either, it may create unnecessary tension later.

28

Managing Multi-Layers of Managers

The thing about managers is that they are smart (most of the time). Managers are in a difficult position because they are the liaison between upper management (Executive Level) and their staff – line employees included. They key to managing managers is to make sure they are all on the same page. Any conflicting instructions or goals will complicate and/or create tension and chaos through competing ideas. That's not to say competition is not good, but you certainly want it somewhat friendly, but definitely civil. Definitive direction must be set during detailed and strategic management meetings, then reinforced in one-on-one or micro meetings. Try to look at:

- The challenges that your managers face. Although it is their job to work through challenges...it's your job to know their challenges and guide.
- During your meetings, the one-on-one's especially, listen carefully and direct in a way that keeps them on the rails. Your managers have to be on the same page.

- Ask your managers how they see their position/ responsibilities and how they foresee accomplishing the tasks and goals. It gives them an opportunity to say this aloud, hence, committing to themselves, and gives you an opportunity to align them.
- Be aware and prepared that your managers may not always be aligned. But, this is a case for knowing your managers. Know their strengths, know their weaknesses, support where/when necessary, develop them for the sake of the company. Manage your relationship with them through reason and confidence, not through fear and demoralization.

29

Don't Wait... Be a Decision Maker Now

You know how it works, someone else is making the decisions, but you know that you can make that decision better and with more efficiency. Well, that may be the thought, but solutions don't always come in single wraps. Your boss made that decision based on information he/she had at the time. Nevertheless, how do you become relevant now in decision making?

- Think through issues at hand and take initiatives that will show your ability to think outside your departments priorities - only.
- Know what your boss is working towards and propose solutions ahead of time. Staying ahead shows initiative and forward thinking.
- Look at others in key positions...How are they dressing, how are they conducting themselves in meetings, how are the behaving inter-office/with colleagues? The idea is not to emulate to the point of

copy, (you are who you are) but, to have an idea of how others see things...to have an idea of how they've conducted themselves to reach a point where they are making key decisions.

- Read biographies of people you admire.

30

Consistency with Subordinates

Subordinates, whether managers or line employees are equally impacted by the facial expressions, moans, verbal jabs, inattention, looking at your cell, etc. from their bosses. The consistency with how you are perceived by your subordinates is not only important to the trust they have in you, but also how they feel perceived by you.

- When dealing with subordinates be careful about how and what you say about others - coming from a manager it spreads quickly and may disable your credibility. Be aware of your subtleties...people pick up on these and quickly become judgmental.
- Don't talk so much. There's nothing like sitting in front of the boss when s/he's taking up all the air in the room. Being able to finish ones thoughts is important to understanding the whole context.
- Expectations are important...it allows people to be prepared. If they come into your office on Monday and

you're Dr. Jekyll, then Tuesday you're Mr. Hyde, well, they don't know what to expect and can throw the productivity of the meeting off, or quite frankly ruin someone's day. Look, it's not your responsibility to be Mr. Rogers and make everyone's day a happy one, but being a moody boss is not good...or consistent.

- Try not to make faces and noises - as in an annoyed smirk, or a loud breath, or a dismissive wave of the hand about an idea. It sends a signal of disrespect and disinterest that may be demoralizing.

Having that expectation of consistency with your subordinates values that perception of themselves that increases their interest in what they do, hence, they are more productive. No one likes to be devalued and your consistency with your subordinates, (guaranteed) will give you that reputation. Try not to glance at your cell or commuter either...

31

Driving your Point

You have ideas on how to increase productivity, service or an outright different way of dealing with or marketing to your customers – whatever. Or perhaps you have been delegated to by your boss to work on a project. These things should be approached in a certain way:

- First, you need to get your mind wrapped around the idea clearly. There's a goal or end result that you are looking to accomplish – that goal/picture must be in your head, otherwise, how do you know where you're going.
- Do some contemplation. Ponder and work through issues and variables that may arise. Who are the key players? What departments will be impacted? Who are the beneficiaries? Who has a stake in having this succeed, or fail? In other words work through these things so you can defend your position and your results. Remember English Composition in grade

school? Introduction, Body, Ending. When addressing your boss or when pitching your idea it should be developed in this manner – it tells the listener you put serious thought into it in an organized manner.

- Never forget the financial importance of your idea or project. Businesses are interested in the ROI. How is this going to save money or make money for the company? If it's a value added position, there has to be an assumption on how it will benefit financially either in the short or long term.

Although the devil is in the details don't complicate or over explain issues. Most people (especially your boss) do not have time for a long story. Simplify and give key points. Remember that you must be able to defend your end result. The more thought you've put into it the better prepared and confident you will be when others (including your boss) challenge you and/or try to punch holes in your idea or project.

32

Your Presence

How you carry yourself and the way you are perceived by others is critical to your growth. There are those that would be critical of this statement pointing out that it's your performance alone that should dictate your growth. Well, that's nice and all, but sorry...does not work that way. Businesses are in the business of presentation and you as part of that presentation require a certain behavior that represents the businesses/organizations perception to others/customers. How do you affect this?

- Project yourself in a confident manner. Place yourself (your mindset) in that place and act the part. Do not gossip, do not step on others, do not kiss _ _ _.
- Project yourself in the way you dress. Wearing unfitted clothing or slopping something together that passes for businesses wear is not good enough. You've heard the saying... "Dress for Success", well it's true. Others (especially your bosses) can see how you project

yourself. They may not compliment or comment, but the perception is there, it is made.

- Project your stance. Keep your eyes still, don't bite your nails, don't pick at your nails, don't move your body all over the chair, if you're standing don't move all over the office...you get the picture. Poise – look it up.

- Project your speech. When you speak to others always be civil and professional. Try not to slang so much and don't over smile all the time...people will think there's something wrong with you.

No one will ever tell you that you're not qualified for a promotion or position because you don't carry yourself properly. It's something you must know on your own. There are classes/seminars you can take, there are ways to practice... what's important is that your presentation is presentable. The subtleties of your presence speak volumes about you.

33

Think Different

How many times have you heard... "We need new blood" or "Come on team, think!" New ideas are what most organizations are looking for. It gives them a competitive edge. The problem is that an entrenched management and staff without a creative culture will stagnate. Try and think different by:

- Exercise different solutions on issues. For example, day-in-day-out you're making decisions about things/ challenges that arise. You no doubt have a default solution because you've seen this challenge before and through your experience know that this particular way is the best way. If you stop for a moment and consider alternatives, it may help build a more creative solution. This can actually be adopted on a much larger scale as well... For example, how your team or organization handles some of the bigger issues that can have a much deeper effect on the direction of the organization.

- Always be aware of what your competitors are doing. If they are doing things the same way you are – then what's the difference in the customer's eyes? On the other hand, maybe they are doing something you're not and that may be one of the reasons your organization is, "Looking for new blood."

Always be looking on how to improve the customer experience. That's what your organization needs. Do not be afraid to suggest/recommend new ideas...it shows that you are thinking differently and have a creative mind. Ignore the nay sayers...your office is full of them. By thinking different, different things happen, creative things happen.

34

Being too Optimistic

Having a positive and optimistic attitude is good, it's contagious, it allows for creative thinking, it gives an impression of confidence and so on. However, it can be demoralizing and counterproductive as well. Let's break this into two parts.

- When giving your team a project and relate to them that it is a fairly simple task or suggest to them that it's easy work, it can actually have the opposite effect of what you're trying to accomplish. Unforeseen issues come up in every project/task and allowing your team to make mistakes and learn from them is good management. Having them feel as if they couldn't handle something simple (because your optimism gave that impression) will sap their efforts next time.
- Let's take the analogy of a farmer growing strawberries. You can imagine him looking at the fields and hoping and wishing for those strawberries to grow with

his/her mantra of, "the strawberries will come…". Well, the strawberries won't come unless the farmer does something to help them come – plant the seeds, water, protect from insects, etc. In other words the farmers hope and optimism that something good is going to come out of the fields without actually doing something to make it happen is just that, hope and optimism. It does not work without doing something.

Optimism involves strategy and planning. It works when you have an outcome in mind, but there must be work towards that outcome with a deliberate sense of vision to the pieces involved to make it work.

35

Dealing with a Collapsed Norm

It is demoralizing to be in a situation where something you've been use to begins to collapse. The toughest part about this is, well, everything. The leadership may have changed or the company out right sold, etc. Whatever it is the environment that ensues can be stressful and dealing with it takes strength, grace and a wily approach.

Your boss may be pitting you against one or more of your colleagues, your colleagues striving for relevance and survival begin to turn on each other, or new blood ups the tempo or competition within your sphere/responsibilities. It's not easy, but try these things:

- Discuss with your colleagues the changes and situation you are all experiencing. Sticking together is more productive than dog-eat-dog...no one survives then.

- Regardless of the attempts by colleagues to work against you, work with them instead – this will help defuse any insecurities or mal-intents they may have.
- In a very calm, diplomatic and constructive way, explain to your boss how you feel. Try and get a sense of the direction and attempt to educate your boss on what you do exactly. Make sure it's not in a complaining manner.

Keeping in mind that the norm can change is a good start to any position/job. Understanding that shareholders, partners, executives, owners can be fickle and anxious for change is always a possibility...and is actually more the norm today than it was yesteryear.

36

Overdoing it in your Role

Whether you've started a new job or have a new boss... easy does it. First and foremost the most obvious thing to others (especially your boss) is when you are trying too hard to prove yourself. There are ways to approach your role and still shine.

- Back off and assess what is going on around you. There may be others fighting for the spotlight and why put yourself in that fray. If you've just started a new job do the same...you should know what's going on around you before jumping into decisions or commitments that may boomerang back to you.
- There is always the unexpected, expect it. By over compensating in your role you risk being perceived as reckless. Your performance is based on knowledge, experience and reason. Use those attributes to balance yourself.
- The culture of an organization will always slow you down. Organizations by nature do not like change.

Any attempt to force procedures or policies through that are not popular will remain unpopular.

- Over doing it by over working looks like you are over doing it by over working. It's silly. Your confidence should be enough for you and your boss...unless you don't know what you are doing.

Over doing it in your role comes from the lack of confidence in your abilities. Business' roles in a deliberate day-by-day momentum. Your awareness of your responsibilities in your role and your bosses reasonable expectations of you should not require you to run around looking busy or try and prove yourself like a child before Christmas.

Now, let's put this into perspective. We're talking about over doing it, hence, making mistakes and/or being perceived as an over promisor and under-deliver(er). Working hard is important to your role as you are developing your career and building on your experience. Earning your title and growth is still based on hard work - but when working hard, work smart. Long hours for the sack of impression will not work for you.

37

Your Unfocused Strategy

Once your idea is set, you build the chronology and mechanics of the idea in your head with your goals, then you begin the processes of strategizing. As your thoughts are moving through this process the images are apparent and you're ready to go. But, not really. Having an image in your head is one thing...managing the process is another. Your mind has a tendency to skip through some fairly important details or aspects that may be crucial to the success of a project or strategic direction of an organization. So, consider:

- Study the details of the path that the strategy will take and attempt to project forward areas that may create bumps along the way. Do not attempt to please all along the way...customers or employees. It's a sure way to spread the strategy too thinly and there's your unfocused strategy.
- Be careful not to apply the same strategy from area to another. In other words, your strategy may have

worked at company A, but more than likely will not work at company B. This is where studying the details of the path come in. Every environment is different and the application of your strategic focus needs to be clear to that environment. We're talking about the details here...an overall strategy is different, for example; we want to generate 10% additional revenue for the next quarter. That's the overall goal – the devil is in the details.

- Choosing your battles is critical to the success of your strategy. Don't get stuck in an unnecessary power play or on something that can be bypassed and either revisited or ignored all together. Chances are that you won't have to revisit certain battle grounds because the area of contention may change on its own due to conformity of the overall strategy or simply become irrelevant to the overall strategy.

Remember (and any general will tell you this) that the best layout battle plan or strategy will go amok. The trick is anticipation and preparation.

38

Setting an Example of Work and Personal Life

How many times have you heard, "Who has time?" Your mindset is very important here because it's easy to fall into a pattern or routine that restricts the time you have for your personal life. Work is necessary and it's important to apply yourself in a way that encourages growth and quality performance. What is not necessary is sacrificing your personal life for your work life. Your subordinates are watching... and if you mismanage your time, they will mismanage theirs or a misunderstanding of what is expected of them will surface. Then you will have problems.

- If your subordinates see you as nervous and insecure about your job/performance as you stay late at work often, then they will be nervous and insecure about their job/performance. The attitude will change to that of pressure.

- Know that you and your subordinates have a life outside work. When at the office, yes...concentrate on work and perform. You cannot leave work early (for your personal life) and show a good example to your subordinates if you are not performing.
- It's important to engage your subordinates about their work performance and efforts as well as set the example and encourage them to have a life outside the office.

Obviously there are different levels of intensity and management levels that require different time management of your work and personal life. What's important is that you are aware of your influence and work habits that others see. It's not just your subordinates watching...your boss is watching too. Remember, if you cannot get done what you should be able to get done in a normal work day, then there is something wrong – either with your work habits/skills or the expectations from your own boss. Either way, you need to set an example and balance your time.

39

Others Perceptions

What do your boss or colleagues think of you? What's their perception of you? Do you care? Well, whether you care or not has much to do with how you perceive yourself really. If you are secure in how you conduct yourself, secure in your performance, have confidence in your experience, then you probably don't care much how others perceive you. This is good...except if you're looking for opportunities and others perceptions of you block your advance.

- Understand always that you are marketing yourself. Be aware of how you present projects and ideas in front of your boss and colleagues. Stay true to facts and your work...and that perception will get out there.
- Is there someone you trust (and that trusts you)? Someone you admire as a colleague? The two of you (or three) can advance each other's ideas and accomplishments by promoting each other. Not in an obvious way where others question your motives, but

in subtle ways during meetings, outings, discussions at the water cooler, etc.

- If in doubt on how to manage how others perceive you... simply be yourself and do your work.

The problem with how others perceive you is that it's based on judgments. People have a tendency to judge immediately and to change the judgment (perception they have) takes work – if you care. Flying straight, saying less, respecting others and concentrating on your responsibilities will usually give you an even keel with regard to others perception of you. More importantly, care more about the perception your boss and colleagues have of you - the ones that will help you with opportunities and advance your ideas, not the people that are vying for position or have another agenda, hence, their perception of you is skewed.

40

Understanding your Position/Placement

How do you see your company's position or placement in your market/industry? How do your competitors see you? These are important questions because they have to do with concentration of resources and growth. What does this mean exactly?

- In your current capacity as company head, division or department head it is critical that you understand your position within your market. This sounds simple, but applying or allocating company resources (including financial) into something that you do not have a complete and thorough understanding of... is a waste of resources.
- In order to be competitive and grow your positioning as a follower or innovator should be understood. In other words, if you are competing for market share, what do your competitors offer that you don't... and vice-versa. Must you follow them because they

have the financial/or overall resources giving them a competitive edge or are you an innovator in new segment? Either way you need to know this so you are not only allocating your resources properly, but also so you are not placing your company in an uncompetitive position moving in a direction that you are out resourced in.

- Be careful what you don't know. Just because you may see an opportunity in the market does not mean it does not exist, but even if it does not exist a much larger and more nimble competitor may shift its resources to this opportunity and take away your market share.

La-da-da-ing along is a recipe for non-relevance. If you don't know your place with regard to your competitors and customers you are doomed for mediocrity and non-growth. The key is know why and where you exist in the market place always.

41

To Do or Not To Do

Let's apply this in two ways. A new boss comes in. You start a new job and you're the boss.

In any industry when a new boss is brought in they usually have a mandate to shake things up a bit and make changes. The idea is to loosen up bad habits, policies and procedures that may be in place. It's not a bad strategy and you've heard the expression, change is good. A few things to consider.

- In 1921, 1945, 1982 and maybe 2003 a policy of fear to motivate was okay. Today it is passé. There is nothing like fear to suppress morale and creativity. When someone loses confidence due to fear of losing one's job – look out...not only does it lower morale, but it's contagious. No one wants to come to work then, and when they are at work they are less creative and more robotic in their efforts.

- Wait. Whatever the mandate, wait. To jump into a new position and begin changes immediately without consideration of what the variables are is a recipe for heavy resistance and uncertainty. Growth is difficult under normal circumstances, never mind when a dark cloud is hanging over everyone. This does not mean you have to wait a year before making changes and working on your mandate...it simply means assess and understand all the parts involved, hence driving the changes with allies and motivated staff.

- A positive strategy is a win-win strategy. This does not mean you bring in donuts every morning and sing, everything will be alright... but, there is no benefit to reducing the change strategy or mandate to a point of people feeling intimidated and/or worthless. This is why leadership and management skills are important. Balancing requires skill.

This is not to say that changes have to be hunky-dory and we should all just get along, etc. Discharges happen for a reason, change happens for a reason, but, it's the intricacies and strategic planning of the changes that count. Demanding that your managers and employees meet performance standards is critical to your organizations competitiveness. There is a big difference between being engaged in a way that pulls your resources together and coming in as a hammer simply making people feel bad. The first strategy promotes cooperation, innovation, interest, responsibility, obligation, worth, etc. The second promotes, low morale, lazy thinking, 9 to 5 mentality, reduced productivity and ultimately organizational slowdown.

42

What to get out of a Meeting

Well, in many cases what you want to get out of a meeting is just that, get out of it. However, they do serve a purpose and are necessary. So, the question becomes, what would you like to get out of the meeting? You want to come out of it with a gain, with a win on your points and agenda. We are always negotiating... whether it's what you're having for dinner or what direction your company will take, it's a matter of discussion and you have an opinion or reason as to why it should be a certain way. Let's not panic here, this does not mean you throw a tantrum because you cannot get your way, it simply means that you should know what you want to get out of a meeting so you are not pushed or pulled in a direction that is not consistent with your thoughts on it.

- Meetings should always have an agenda. If they do not, (especially one-on-one's) look out... this is a perfect way for the Inviter to ambush you. No agenda means that they have their agenda clear and the meeting will be more about directives.

- You should always take a few moments before a meeting – pause, think about the agenda (provided there is one) and focus on your points, but especially what you want to gain from it. Taking a deep breath before you walk in... keeping in mind to have an open mind, but that you need to get something out of it helps immensely. Your thoughts need to be clear and sharp that it's a negotiation you are walking into, not just a meet and greet.

- Having points before you go into a meeting will help you stay focused on what you want to accomplish and gain. If you walk in without an idea of what you want... be prepared to be delegated to – especially if the other attendees or the Inviter have a strong/ aggressive manner.

Remember that it is always a negotiation and you must be focused on your points in order to come out of the meeting feeling as if you gained something. Again, otherwise you are sheep-ing in someone else's direction. And of course all negotiations should be a win-win. Just as you gain something, the other party should gain as well.

43

Creativity's Tone

The thing about creativity is that it needs space. In today's more constrained, more rules, more security, more litigious, more etc. workplace, it is difficult to unleash those that are best poised to bring creativity to your organization. That can put you in an uncompetitive position. Other constraints come from un-visionary or too conservative ownership, board, leadership... Same end result.

- First and foremost you need to find ways around the obstacles that are constraining your creative staff. Ideas are not enough to stay competitive. Implementation, hence budget is imperative. How do you balance this? You need to show your boss clarity in ROI and clarity in purpose. You can't be seen as wasting resources on ideas that go nowhere. Be specific as to the reasons and results.
- Your direction and vision is critical in keeping the creative process tamed to the organization's mission.

Your creative people/staff should be looking over the horizon constantly – what trends are taking place, and watching competitors - what are they offering?

- The obstacles and constraints are in place for a reason – whatever that may be. Having an environment that is conducive to creativity is the key. You need to find ways to breakdown the barriers without bringing negative attention to your department or team. The best way to do this is to show results.

The most important thing about a creative tone is the morale of your staff. Suppress morale, suppress creativity and productivity. It's important to understand that there are other smart people in the room – tap that.

44

Distrusting the Process

There's nothing like sitting in your office and watching a colleague walk by time-after-time and go right into the boss's office – then another colleague… You are not sure why, but whatever it is you are not being included. What happens then is you begin to form an anxiety and anxiousness, then distrust. Why? Because you are feeling left out of something - so you think. When the process itself is off it throws off other things. This is where gossip forms, untruths form, conjecture forms, disgruntle-ness forms etc. As a leader you should be aware of this and create an environment of straight forwardness and trust.

- Be cognoscente of your body language and facial expressions. When you are looking away or walking away you are showing a disinterest.
- In meetings make sure to be open about the process and upcoming projects and who will be working on them and why.

- Have the pertinent people involved in the project meetings instead of allowing the information to just trickle down. The person that it trickles down to will be out of the loop and distrustful of the motives and direction.
- Understand the psychology of your subordinates and colleagues. Asking people to trust you is not enough – they must be shown.

The distrust of the process happens (especially) anytime there is change afoot. People become very alert, attuned and hyper sensitive to what is going on around them. They become fearful, defensive, protective of their environment - and of course they are... why wouldn't they if the information is not forthcoming and the boss is less than open. It's not just a matter of making a speech, it is a matter of paying attention to what you are doing and understanding the effect on others in the office. The more open you are about changes, projects, etc. the less opportunity for insecurities to fester and a culture of distrust ensue.

45

Creating Intrigue

This has to be one of the most frustrating things in the work place... that is, the ones that look to create intrigue either deliberately or as it may simply be part of their personality. Either way it creates tension, unnatural competition, dissension, worry and most importantly wasted thought and time. This type of behavior is motivated by only two things, fear and insecurity. When a colleague or subordinate begin this type of tone it is important to back off from the conversation, lest be dragged into an uncomfortable situation.

- You can immediately identify this behavior by the tone of voice and direction in which the deliverer is speaking. If it sounds like gossip then it is gossip.
- By allowing the behavior to go unabated, is to allow the intrigue to grow. Unintended falsities and untruths grow from rumors. It is best to remove yourself as a receiver.
- Colleagues/subordinates that create intrigue create unnecessary drama within any organization and is

a key morale killer if allowed to persist. It delivers an unserious and dampened environment by trading confidence for concern.

When others discuss others and complain about behaviors, situations, motivations, duties, etc. they are creating and fomenting negatives throughout the work environment or organization. It breeds distrust and suspicion about others that can be damaging to both reputations and motives. It's important to realize that what is being said is coming from a very personal place and is specific to how that person views things. When discussions move in a direction of fact, seriousness, honesty, integrity, trust... without tearing down others or attempting to create an idea/intrigue as to another's thought process, then the collaboration and cooperation is more direct and free of gossip (or baseless rumors) allowing for a clear and predictable work environment.

These are a lot of words for something that can be summed up as someone that starts rumors and talks about others in a conspirator way and plays everything off as if they are an innocent victim of the information coming to and from them. Not.

So, how do you deal with this as a boss/leader? Well, it depends if you are in a small or large organization. In a large organization you should attempt to nip the creator of intrigue in the bud. This includes speaking with the originator, then referring to HR if the behavior does not improve...as it is a behavioral issue with repercussions. In a small organization it is much easier. The behavior should not be tolerated in the least and removed/discharged fairly quickly as the damage can be much worse and rapid.

46

Hesitation

In business, hesitation can be costly, both financially and competitively. It can also retard the process and timing of projects. It's a simple matter of understanding your goal and/or numbers and having the confidence that your decision is the right one. Yes, easier said than done. There is a difference between being impulsive and having thought through something allowing you to overcome any hesitation in your decisions.

- When you hesitate, you are questioning yourself. It's okay to question yourself, but not when a quick decision is required. It's a akin to pulling onto a highway from the on-ramp and breaking instead of merging. If you are breaking then you are unsure of your decision.
- When you hesitate, others question you and themselves. Information is vital to making quick decisions, otherwise you are winging it and that's

where mistakes happen. That's also impulsive. Your subordinates and colleagues can tell if your quick decisions are based on experience and knowledge. This is because of their confidence in you and their own reasoning that the decision is good.

- When you hesitate, a void is created. When a void is created something will fill it. When something fills it, it is difficult to change as the process moves forward and other decisions are being made based on the last.

As a word hesitation basically means unsure. Hesitate while you are crossing the street and the car just misses you, or the car hits you. What you have done is not assess the situation quickly enough and not calculated the risks quickly enough either. By hesitating, whether it is because you are being cautions by experience or because something seems off, you in essence allow the context to change where then you are chasing/searching for the right decision and that right decision may have passed. It allows for the fomenting of variables that you did not consider before. When you don't hesitate, but have the confidence and the determination to watch and control and adjust the process of your decision, that is the true necessity for a leader as timorous hesitation is not.

47

Have an Idea Where You Are Headed

There had to be a time when you started your career or when you were in school and you were looking ahead thinking about where you would be and what you would be doing 5 or 10 years hence in your career. For most, you are not where you thought you would be. There is a reason for that...some of it may be due to unforeseen circumstances, but most of it is due to a lack of strategy. Your professional life takes planning and strategic maneuvering and risks.

- Look at where you are today. Is it where you thought you would be? Are you doing better than your expectations or nowhere near them? Regardless of where you are you need to have a professional strategy going forward. If you do not you are at the behest of others. You are floating.
- The routine, the mundane, the over and over again that you perform everyday – that is the way you have no idea where you are headed. This is not to say a routine

is not good...we need routines for consistencies and some expectation, but to enhance your professional standing/position things need to be shaken up and a deliberate focused strategy created.

- It is a step-by-step process and no guarantee that your strategy will work, but at a minimum you are in somewhat control of your own professional destiny.

Your ability to think, dream, plan where you want to be gives you a sense of purpose and independence. Your professional career should have more to do with you and your thoughts about it than with someone else (your boss perhaps) that you are trying to impress. Having the confidence that you know what you are doing and having strength in your stance keeps your forward thinking focused. Have an idea where you are headed...because if you don't, others are the directors of your destiny.

48

The Hiring Balance

The process of hiring employees can be a mundane and routine exercise yielding less than qualified employees, or at a minimum employees shoved into a position for the sake of getting bodies in there. The problem is that these employees just came from another interview with the same process as yours. It is like a merry-go-round for both you and them. Your hiring process must be targeted, concise and deliberate in its criteria... because that is where the fit and influence of a company's culture begins.

- Where you recruit from suggests the quality of candidates you will receive. Whether they are from a recruiter, recommendation from within, or an online application process the screening should be vigorous to your points and needs. This is not to say 3 background checks is needed, but that the details of the candidate's qualifications are looked at beyond the surface of what is on the paper/resume.

- The strategy of the screener, whether HR or recruiter should be such as to have a clear and coordinated do's and don'ts in order to consolidate the screening process (better before a candidate comes in) so as to avoid time wasting, hence costs.

- The culture you have or want to instill starts with the recruiting. Again, this goes to where your candidates are coming from. However, the questions you ask during the interview process are so important because that in itself, when the answers come back, are a determining factor of fit. Of course this sounds trivial and obvious, but it is not. Ask the wrong questions and get the wrong candidate. Get the wrong candidate and so goes the merry-go-round, not to mention the wasted time and money. What are the right questions? Well, that is for your executives, board or proprietor to decide...and it should be a serious and well thought-out decision.

- HR should not be your guru of hiring. HR is stuck in the questions of processing and legalities. Your managers and executives, whom also should be versed on the hiring strategies and who will be working with, for, or above the hires' are critical to the process and perhaps the most important element. Too heavy a reliance on HR shows weakness in management skills.

- Having a hiring strategy that fits the culture of your company also helps avoid the biases, nepotism or favoritism that exists when a proper strategy is not set. Watch then as the wrong candidate creates issues, albeit not deliberate, but simply because they were not vetted to the culture properly.

It cannot be overstated the importance of the right questions. The right questions can vet in such a way as to determine if you can work with this person, if your employees can work with this person, if their mindset and attitude are fixed to your company needs, or if the culture is right for them or vice-versa...all bringing together the right person for/in the right job. The alternative is what is discussed in other parts of this book – challenges, problems and unhealthy politics that can be avoided.

49

Line Employee Syndrome

Making the jump from a line employee position to a supervisory/managerial position is a great accomplishment. It is a step in the right direction for future growth in your professional life. In order for this to have happened, others, your boss most of all, must have seen something about you that qualified you. At the point of transition your mindset needs to adjust away from certain aspects of your behaviors and thoughts. How so? Supervisors and managers look at circumstances differently than line employees do with respect to numbers, staffing, staff behaviors, processes and procedures, etc. It is a broader look, companywide. You know you are stuck in that syndrome when:

- You walk into work right on time every day.
- When you are starring at the clock waiting to go home.
- When ask to leave work early because you have a headache.

- You call in sick because you wake up with a stomach ache.
- When you gossip to colleagues about bosses.
- When you gossip to bosses about colleagues.
- When you dress in unfitted or sloppy clothing.
- When you don't take care of your personal hygiene. Mirror, mirror.
- When you don't read up on industry happenings.
- When you have something better to do than being in a meeting where you might learn something.
- When you don't make yourself part of the process to increase productivity.
- When you have complaints, but no solutions.

In other words care why you have been promoted and adjust yourself out of your previous thinking and mindset. Play the part as you work your way up the ladder.

50

Cost Containment

Cost containment is not just a matter of signing off on anything that needs to be purchased. That slows things down and presents inconveniences to the department heads or project managers. It is at the point of, and early in, the process of the decisions where the costs are being effected. It's easy to say, "Let's do this" or "Do that", but this and that have a cost, sometimes residual or recurring. It's akin to shipping a product, then inspecting it – it's already left. The same holds true with expenses. Some of the expenses/costs are value added (these are important) so it is difficult to see a return in tangible terms. But, too much of it and you have costs that are habitual, difficult to track and hard to reel back in. You can't control a cost that you can't see – intangibles.

Before any new policies or procedures are launched the project managers and/or department heads need to determine its value and reasoning. Establishing the need and feasibility by having a direction and understanding the cost. It allows you to control costs, hence ensure that everyone knows the direction and need (or what is not needed). The process or management is called target cost containment. Target cost containment supports the strategy that focuses on productivity.

The bottom line is that costs go up unrealized and the management of these costs needs to be done before, not after. That means at the point of strategy or decision.

The solution is to manage the expenses and whoever is qualified to do it, should do it. Especially in small business as there is more difficulty, less of a financial buffer and sophisticated productivity models that let's say larger companies may have. That means there is less committee and/or checks and balance in place...which is okay if someone is watching expenses diligently.

51

Organizational Change and People

Organizational change has got to go down as one of the most stressful exercises in business. It is filled with emotion, tension, confusion, timorous behaviors, anger, fear, regrets, distractions...the list goes on. As decisions go, Organizational Change is a big one and it requires big boy/girl decisions to be made. This may require discharges, shifting staff to other positions, changing the environment and comfort zone of staff, changes in policy or direction... again, the list goes on. Whatever organizational changes are taking place, the strategy must be well thought-out ahead of time and some real consideration given to existing employees, policies and procedures as they relate to the short and long term goals, lest disorganization ensues. Flying by the seat of your pants while engaged in Organization Change is a recipe for chaos, confusion, dissension, disgruntling behavior, lessoned productivity and bottom line negative impact.

- Guessing and wrong conclusions are afoot because communication about the changes are not upfront. Staff, but especially managers slip into paralysis for lack of clear direction.
- When Organizational Change is afoot morale slips regardless of the intentions. The changes require quick decisions and actions while at the same time demonstrating sincere respect and openness. Nothing like having the feeling that you are unappreciated in your responsibilities and your job is on the line. It's akin to being unable to steer away from the brick wall you are about to hit – except it's in slow motion.
- Poor decisions, poor judgments, poor analysis from your employees will be abundant because they are unsure of… much. During changes, if they are made to feel as if they do not count, then they will not count. One of the real qualities of human beings is that they adapt to change…but only when they are given the resources and information to be a part of the change.

When creating change in your business it is much more productive to have the existing staff as part of the organizational change. Yes, there are instances of mass layoffs that are required (again, a quick decision and action), circumstances of less qualified individuals, de-railers, bloated departments, etc, but the only way you know that is by fully understanding the capabilities, strengths and efforts of those individuals and honing their skills to the changes.

In any organizational change slow and tepid decision making only allows for more confusing and disorganized material to seep in, hence slowing or de-railing the whole change strategy...if there ever was one. Areas that exist don't just go away because an effort to change has started. This refers to culture, policies, procedures, staff...anything. The changes come from deliberate interference and strong, quick decision making. Either the existing staff is part of the change (team) or not. There is a reason for that expression about pulling a Band-Aid off fast - and it's because it does.

52

Your Social Connection

We are social beings...this is obvious in how we look at other on the bus, train, or in our cars, etc., it's obvious when you seek attention from others, it's obvious in everything we do. Because we are social beings we need to connect to others. As a boss this is more critical than you may think.

- When you wake in the morning, go home in the evening and what you do on the weekends is the same thing that everyone else is doing. Your connection to your staff should include things you have in common so they can relate to you.
- Holding your discussions to business only and cloaking yourself in an unnatural stoic disposition will only alienate the people around you. Less pertinent information will reach you as others are not so inclined to speak with you. Not being approachable is not how leaders/bosses get things done. Your influence channels through connections with others.

- Being afraid to connect with your staff because of perceived misinterpretations, perceived legal ramifications, perceived saying the wrong thing is just silly. Yes, conduct yourself in a mature manner that is representative of your position, but don't run around with a face that says, closed.

The point is that you must have a connection with the people you work with. Otherwise your job and theirs becomes a chore for a great part of the day. It is important that your staff feels and sees that you relate to them and that you are approachable. Of course this needs to be done in a way that preserves everyone's privacy, and staff must understand the line between boss and colleague, but allowing yourself to connect will increase productivity by opening the lines of communication and trust.

53

Opinionated Slight

These are those annoying opinions that others have that are not just opinions, but a beneath the radar dig on another. This type of opinion is designed for one thing...bring down another to lift themselves. The reasons why opinionated slights are made is not as important as how to deal with them.

- If you have identified one of these people one way to deal with them is to stay away from any hearsay and gossipy type conversations with them. Engage in a business type conversation only.
- Control the conversation...do not allow it to turn into a subject about others that does not involve facts.
- Reduce your interactions with such people as you will inevitably become a target of the opinionated slights.

Opinionated slight is another term for throwing others under the bus. It comes from fear, impulsiveness and lack of security.

Standing on your own and being confident in your ability to defend or make a point without pulling others into it is a sign of security and confidence.

From a bosses perspective it is usually identified quickly and in most cases will backfire.

54

You are Perishable

Our cemeteries are filled with indispensable people. Remember that the next time you think you are the smartest in the room or that the company cannot do without you. Although this is a harsh statement it is the reality of the business world.

- Continually stay up on your industry happenings. Nothing like being in a meeting and you are caught off guard by something. Being progressive and educated in your industry will at a minimum allow you to stay relevant.
- Always be looking forward. If you were to lose your job today, what would you do tomorrow? This does not mean you should be paranoid about it, but a least be aware.
- What other industry can your current experience be transferred to? Others are reluctant to hire outside their industry, however, if a comparative case is made, it could help.

- Think about what you can do on your own with your experience and talents. Can you start your own business?
- Understanding that there is always movement within an organization and change is a constant... your standing and questions in this environment should be of the utmost importance to you, lest you find yourself in a position of having no position. You are a perishable. Be aware.

55

What is the Solution?

Your mind should be geared to solutions, not just bringing up problems. Even if the solution is not accepted, at a minimum the issue is moving forward as opposed to being stuck in neutral lamenting over a problem.

- If you allow your mind to concentrate on a problem, it will concentrate on the problem and give you little help. As a matter of fact all your mind will do is keep telling you how bad the problem is.
- If you press your thoughts to solutions, your mind will give you solutions. As a matter of fact it will motivate you to move forward.
- Controlling your thoughts on this is imperative. It is the difference between being stuck and lamenting or doing something that gets you closer to solving the problem.

Anybody can sit in a meeting and talk about problems... and perhaps hope for recognition that they have identified a problem. But, the real recognition comes when solutions are presented. Now you are moving forward.

56

Idea Fluidity

What are you thinking about all day? You are probably thinking the same thoughts day-after-day...and between 10:30am and noon you are problem thinking about that big decision – what to have for lunch. What you actually need to do is train yourself to think about ideas... to have ideas. Your ideas create creativity, innovation and when moving fluidly, solutions.

- Don't concentrate or lament so much about what happened yesterday. Force your mind forward and ask yourself questions, like, what if.
- Contemplate issues which will force your mind to think things through. The more questions the better.
- Think about what else... What else can you be doing? What else does the boss want? What else is there, etc...?

As much as it is a cliché, your ideas are only limited by your fear and your fear. Yes, fear blocks everything and anything. When your ideas are fluid you become proficient and mastered in building yourself a business, a promotion... your search for doing.

57

You are not Appreciated

Are your feelings hurt? Waiting around for approval will get you nowhere fast. Remember that the cemeteries are filled with indispensable people. The idea that you should be appreciated or honored for what you have accomplished or the "good" job that you are doing is not going to move you forward. This is not to say that we do not need or should not want to be recognized for what we are doing...hence, why do it in the first place? The point is you need to progress and build on what you are accomplishing, then move on. Don't wait around.

Think for a moment about all the great ideas you have had... what you have put forth and what has come out of that. It could be something or things you have done for a person personally, someone you have helped get a promotion, got a job for, gave away an idea or your idea allowed a solution that made something or saved something/someone... Are you waiting around for the person or situation, whether a boss, friend, circumstance, boyfriend/girlfriend, child, etc. to appreciate and thank you for everything you have done... and they will never forget...? No! Don't wait, move on and keep moving because that is ultimately what makes you grow.

Also remember that most people believe that "they" are responsible for where they are dismissing anything or anyone that has helped them achieve or accomplish the position they are in. Many times they are even resentful. So, how should you react? You shouldn't... move on and keep going because you are not appreciated and your fulfillment should come from within, not from without.

58

Others

In charge of your growth. Well, this cannot be completely avoided as your performance and promotions depend on others. However, if you are not cognoscente of your behavior, disposition, interactions, performance then you are allowing others to judge you in a way that actually dictates your growth and/or direction. So, how does one relate to the other? If you do not know or if your goal is less than clear... others, (meaning the decision makers in your company) make judgments and decisions that inevitably condition your path. In other words, you think that you are performing and doing everything correct... that will lead you to what? Your awareness of what is happening around you and your behavior, disposition, interactions and performance within that context is what will dictate your growth. Being in control of your path so others are not setting it for you is key. How do you do this?

- Be stoic in your approach. Others do not need to know your plans.

- Be patient in your expectations. Getting rich quick and being successful (your definition of successful) quick is not usual. It takes planning and time.
- Be disciplined in your efforts. Again, plan quietly, but strategically.

We all need others... that is the basis of our existence and success. It is how you control your path and how you work to get there based on your idea, not others.

59

That Gut Feeling

Your gut feeling is intuitive for sure. It is a primal defense mechanism that is trying to warn you about something. However, be cautious in your acceptance of what you feel or what you think it is telling you. Your gut feeling is based on previous experiences and can be biased in its message.

This is where logic becomes very useful. Being able to understand what you are feeling exactly and disseminating that information so as not to react impulsively or irrationally, or simply by making the wrong decision based on a fear is imperative.

- Be aware of the bigger picture. What is going on around you that has your gut, hence your mind focusing on a direction?
- Do not make any decisions without all the information. A gut feeling may be based on your insecurities and

you will only make it worse by acting on something with "just a gut feeling."

- Purge the gut feeling as well as you can by not fomenting the thought pattern that is bring you to a conclusion that may not be accurate.

Knowing what you are thinking and minimize your emotions based on gut feelings. Dismiss ideas that a situation exists without proof.

60

When to Just Do It

There is a lot to be said about independence and autonomy. We need guidelines, but I would bet that most of us would just like to be trusted to work alone. "I got it, don't worry."

Well unfortunately it does not exactly work this way for the vast majority of us. So, how do you know when to just do it... without checking with the boss?

- The thing about bosses is that they like independent thinkers. Especially when they have molded these people themselves. Bosses like people that challenge the status-quo as long as it does not conflict with their vision.
- Knowing your bosses reaction and intentions can help immensely. You will know what you can get away with by probing.

- Making sure your actions are within company and legal guidelines gives you leverage to defend your actions later if questioned.

The idea is to not be saddled with asking the boss every time a decision needs to be made...especially remedial ones. When you just do it you show your bosses and colleagues that you are unafraid and a decision maker. Yes, there will be push back at times...nevertheless, just do it.

61

Strategic Meetings

Different than Operations Meetings, Executive Committee Meetings, etc. Strategic Meetings should be designed and conducted in conformity of the overall vision and mission of the company. Unlike other meetings, strategic meetings are deliberate in their focus and dismissive of non-essential discussions that may interfere with that focus. Strategic Meetings are short in duration with key decision makers present providing the opportunity to bulldoze through obstacles as necessary.

- To be effective and to stay on point... the team should be well rehearsed and in sync with each other. No competitive slights should be tolerated. Clear disagreements are healthy to discuss through. Agenda driven disagreements are unhealthy and unproductive.
- The leader must lead. A weak leader driving a strategic meeting is akin to a child tuning the wheel of a car

absent power steering. A strong leader keeps the team and meeting on point with well-defined direction.

- Be prepared for direction adjustments. As obstacles and new information come about it is important that there is flexibility.

Constant strategic meetings allow a company to meet benchmarks and reduces the possibility of issues falling through the cracks or lingering because a key decision has not been made.

A strategy only works when all the components are in place and/or are caught when they fall out of place. Strategic Meetings also keeps your team on the same page with little room for misunderstandings.

62

Understanding the Vision

Understanding the vision is not just a matter of seeing a goal or opportunity and being there. It takes laying the ground work to get there. Understanding ahead of time what is involved in the details and changes to make the vision possible to attain...otherwise it's not a vision, it is a fantasy. The managerial decisions and the communication to those involved in its success are required.

- What are the strategic decisions that need to be worked through? The details of which matter immensely. Everything from the funding to the ROI and everything in between.
- Is the product or service even marketable? What kind of research needs to be done?
- Is that vision thing communicated convincingly to others that are involved? If not, figure out a simple way to explain.

A vision is broad and does not require complicated details upfront. Anytime that happens it scares potentials away. Others need to visualize your vision – literally. And there is no easier way to repel stake holders, your boss or colleagues than over pitching it. Once that is done, then work on the details and questions of your vision.

63

Transition and Change

While in the beginning and middle of organization change, there is the need to adopt and maintain a healthy and productive work environment. Healthy and productive are synonymous. Organizational change needs to be thought through thoroughly with considerations beyond the end result.

As a leader your responsibility is to acknowledge the fact that you are leading others (staff) on a ride they would prefer not to be on. During transition and change there are many unknowns...staff becomes fearful and acts accordingly. Not because they out right do not want change, but because they are unclear of the destination/outcome.

Whatever culture exists before a transition and change are taking place is a result of many years on a clear path... productive or not. The creation of a culture or of a healthy work environment does not happen with an on/off switch.

Therefore, the new direction must consider how the transition and change should take place while preserving the integrity of the very staff you are leading. It requires knowledge and experience of the realities of the present conditions, human behavior, and adjustments of organizational processes. Any changes that take place with a less than thought through agenda or even callous carelessness of the staff being lead ultimately leads do lower productivity and suppressed behavior.

In simple English, no one likes to come to work and experience an unsure, unhealthy and stressful work environment. The toll it takes on individuals is heavy. Transition and change is best served when done in an open, commutative and engaging manner. Leaders have an obligation and responsibility to structure and manage transition and change by preserving their staff's integrity and value.

The first sentence began with beginning and middle and no end as once it is the end it is too late.

64

AWES

Do you suffer from Annoyed With Everyone Syndrome (AWES)? Well, this is something that can be treated, but it takes real discipline and understanding. The frustration level of highly productive individuals having to put up with everyone else can set you off into a mood that is hardly – happy. Some ways to treat AWE...

- Retreat and think for a few moments. Control your thoughts. Understand the complexities of so many people involved having different motives, different agendas, different understanding of the world (situation) you/we are in.
- Relax yourself and direct without an emotional disposition, hence giving away your AWE.
- Try and be proactive in your efforts in an effort to control circumstances. This is where strategic focus is required. Although it will not eliminate barriers,

carelessness, interference, etc. from others, but at a minimum you will expect such.

Remember something... The world is filled with others that will get in your way, but you need those same people to get things done. Balance.

65

Expected Course/Direction

It's all about effective management which includes communication. When employees are behaving in a loose or uncaring manner... they've lost their direction, or they never had one. Regardless of an organizations policies with regard to benefits or the lack there of, the employees understanding and inclusion of an organizations course and direction is critical to that organizations competitiveness.

- Attempting a command and control type management structure does little except to give orders that squeezes or demands a specific course of action, hence everyone and everything around that command and control needs to shift and gravitate towards. This may have worked in 1903, but not today.
- Loose and uncaring behavior comes from the lack of an expected goal. If the direction of the company is not made clear to the people that are supposed to be a part of making the goals possible/achievable then

inefficient behavior becomes the norm. This type of employee behavior is an intangible... you don't see it until the end of the month and even then a wondering goes on as to what is wrong or how we can do better. The simple answer... employees need the expectation in course and direction.

- Managing in a way that gives your employees that expectation allows you to spend less time putting out fires that originated from a less than clear understanding. Attempting to control the process of employees that don't know something is akin to a ship without a compass – it will get there, but slowly. And that is where and how efficiency is lost.

When all are clear and aware of the course and direction of the organization, all move with a similar purpose. Without it a lot of redundant management is necessary and that equates to time and cost.

66

Identifying the Driven, Contentious, Conscientious

You come into the office everyday (or whatever that may be) and either you are looking or waiting on that one employee that will impress you enough that you're confident in giving them more work – or more responsibility.

- There is the driven employee that is full of ambition. This type of person has a need to move forward and get things done. If they are identified early enough and your organization is in a position to motivate and groom this person(s), then by all means it should be done. They will bore easily if they do not see advancement or if they are pigeon holed in a position that is less than active.
- There is the contentious employee that most err in seeing the benefit of such. This is a person that is anxious and looking for things to keep them busy. They are bored where they are and need goals to

aspire to and to achieve. Their contentiousness comes from an intolerance of inefficient processes. Find this persons niche and interest and watch them perform.

- There is the conscientious employee that is easily overlooked. This person has a strong emotional attachment to the larger picture and the details of getting things right is high on their mind. This type of person identifies issues that may have long term repercussions. They are a good balance in today's get it done now environment.

Of course as with every employee the right talent and balance must be evident. However, a leader's responsibility is to find those strengths and/or weakness and exploit them for both the organization and that individual.

67

A Conscience in Conflict

How do you balance yourself when your job and your conscience conflict with each other? This goes to the other question of whether or not you are happy where you are. This can mean a myriad of things, from your personality conflicting with the culture of an organization to your simply not being happy with the/your direction. How do you know and how do you deal with this?

First and foremost if you are experiencing some sort of conscience conflict you are probably in the wrong job. Now, the problem here is that it is not so easy to simply pick-up and go. Some people can do this because they have fewer personal responsibilities or obligations such as children, mortgage, etc. For those, I would suggest extracting yourself from your current position and seek something you will excel in, hence where your interests really lay. Honestly, if you have a conflict you are not doing anyone any good...not the organization and certainly not yourself.

However, if you are not in the best of flexible positions, you will need to take a more strategic direction. Your thoughts need to be in a contemplative mode as to whether there is a real or perceived conflict. In other words if your personality is in conflict with the culture, how can you adjust to assimilate? Or is that the crux of it? You just cannot assimilate nor do you want to. In this case you will have to change your state/mind-set, your goals, your attention, your motivations, and your habits... This is because you cannot stay someplace where this type of strong conscience conflict exists...it will wear on you, stress you and ultimately change you in a way that will impact your success/happiness later. The challenge is managing your time and efforts to find something else or to do something else - perhaps your own business.

Now, this is not about someone working on a fruit farm and the insecticides offend them... that's a real conscience conflict and they should work someplace else, period. We're talking about a personality that does not get along with a certain organizational culture and/or their professional direction. This goes to a discomfort to the point of not wanting to go to work because of the work environment – whatever that may be.

So, the decision has to be either, get out because you do not belong and you have the flexibility to do so, or plan (create a strategy – written) on how you will get out. Talking to the boss will do nothing... a conscience conflict is within, not without.

68

Sunday Anxiety Syndrome

You know how it is… Friday has come and your plans for the weekend are set. You're having a nice relaxed or adventurous time…then Sunday comes. You begin to think about work and what you will need to work on tomorrow, what you forgot to do, what is due, the heavy thought of 5 more days of work ahead… This occurs mostly Sunday evenings. You are not alone. Many suffer from Sunday Anxiety Syndrome and it can ruin your last weekend day off. How do you cope with this? Is there a cure?

- The most obvious thing you can do is have a distraction. However, even with a distraction the gaps in your activity will allow your thoughts of tomorrow to surface. The trick is, know what you are thinking and keep your mind deliberately focused on something else.
- Preparing things for Monday on Friday will help. Anticipating and planning in advance for that day will

give you a sense of preparedness that will give you a calm and self-psychological advantage knowing your Monday is settled.

- The, it-is-what-it-is attitude will help too. Think of it as dirty dishes... even if you wash them today, there will be more tomorrow. In other words a more lackadaisical approach of not caring so much, (but, we know you do) and getting in the mindset that you will just deal with it tomorrow.

So, there you have it. It's really a matter of getting into the habit of, remember-to-remember not to allow the anxiety to become a dominate thought.

69

Your Lack of Confidence

Where does that come from? Your interactions with others maybe? Perhaps your boss's attitude towards you? A lack of experience? First things first...you have to be able to identify its source. Where is that feeling coming from? What is it? A lot of it has to do with caring what others think or may think. The most important thing is to be comfortable with your own thoughts. Remember that just because another person says it is so, does not necessarily make it so. The strength of your mindset that you need to employ is significant in overcoming a lack of confidence. The comfort level that you must have in yourself must be from that of courage - not with arrogance, but with humility. Build your confidence by...

- Don't care so much what others think. Be strong in your convictions, your conduct, your integrity, and your beliefs - what you have an understanding to be, is yours. You do not need to convince anyone else, nor do you need to be convinced.

- Steer conversations to your comfort zone.
- If someone else is an expert in a subject, let them speak.
- It is better to keep your mouth shut in situations and have people think you don't know a subject, than to open your mouth and confirm it to them. It's akin to testifying on your own behalf and convincing the jury you are guilty. You should have stayed quiet.
- Read. And when you finished reading, read some more.
- Conduct yourself in a congenial manner. Nothing says you know less and that you are insecure than being rude.
- Talk to people in their eyes.
- Remember everyone has an opinion. Your opinion can't be wrong.
- Don't be afraid. Fear paralyzes confidence.

These are just a few examples on building your confidence. Others perceive and judge you on your confidence. Unfortunately it is not something that can be switched on like a switch... it needs constant thought and practice. Building knowledge in a variety if subjects allows you to speak confidentially amongst others.

The key is to not speak about something or do something that you may be pushed back on. The biggest confidence killer is being corrected and/or shunned. Build on your strengths and confidence in areas you are fluid in. Poise is always better than injecting yourself into an unknown area.

70

Unqualified Boss

If you are an unqualified boss, then the people you manage will be unqualified. There are many types of bosses (managing styles) and the key to their success, hence the success of the organization and subordinates rides high on the boss's ability to manage effectively with qualified experience and judgment.

What employees are usually interested in is gaining experience, knowledge and advancement. If the boss (or leadership) has little or no interest in developing employees, the result is that the higher echelons of management are forced to micro-manage which results in slowing the overall results, to include project delays, creative dissipation, and innovative retardation.

An unqualified boss, one that creates dissension, forms clicks, does not reason with subordinates, is not consistent, lacks coaching skills, does not encourage healthy collaboration, ignores hierarchy and limits support will inevitably create a culture of fear and a retraction of talent. Nothing slows an organization more than an unqualified boss looking to compensate through micro-management. A chaotic work process ensues.

- A qualified boss is responsible for understanding the psychology of their workforce.
- A qualified boss is responsible for understanding the strengths and weaknesses of their employees and being able to identify placement of such.
- A qualified boss steers and encourages direction that promotes consistency, creativeness, innovation and a healthy work environment.
- A qualified boss understands the demographic shifts taking place within the work environment and adjusts internal organization procedures to meet the needs of talent.

An unqualified boss is not only identified by poor financial results, but very importantly their inability to manage employees overall and setting up an environment that allows for those poor financial results in the first place.

71

You have a Doubt

This is simple... when you have a doubt, pause. It is different than a gut feeling which is based more on analytical considerations about something. A doubt is a question. Does this combination of clothing work? Should I say something to the boss? The answers are, no, change your clothing, and no, don't say anything to the boss. The urge is to overwhelm the doubt with justification because deep down you want to wear that combination and you want the boss to know what you are thinking. But, the doubt you have is telling you to pause and to think about this a little more.

The feeling of doubt is so strong that it can give you discomfort all day, hence effecting your confidence.

When in doubt, do not act or speak... pause and adjust to the circumstances your doubt is pointing at.

72

Understanding your Equilibrium

Your comfort zone is directly connected to your performance. We all have an equilibrium that allows us to balance ourselves within certain conditions and within those conditions we perform based on that balance. How do you know when your equilibrium is off?

- Anxiety... about your job. If you have that constant strong feeling in your chest then you are out of your comfort zone. Your equilibrium is off.
- You are lost... about your responsibilities. If unsure of what you are doing and why, then you are unbalanced in your position. Your equilibrium is off.
- Discomfort about your value... to the organization. If you are feeling undervalued and not understanding the direction of the organization, your equilibrium is off.

Bottom line, it is not just about feeling sorry for yourself because you are not in the dream job you anticipated. It is about your ability to balance yourself within the context of your job/position whereas you are able to grow, feel valued, be comfortable, appreciate the environment, and respect the leadership's efforts and direction.

If you are unable to perform your job efficiently and there is a constant annoyance or gnawing at your conscience, this can have a direct effect on your confidence causing you to hesitate, question yourself, and slow your growth. Not every place is for everyone. It is a decision you have to make as to where you want to be.

73

Understanding the Company

Direction, goals, leadership, objectives, transitions, changes, politics, nuances... are all things you should be keeping an eye on at work. Being aware of your surroundings and understanding the company you work for can only help you make better and faster decisions later.

- Direction: What direction has your company taken in the last year, month, or week? Was it communicated to you? If not, you should try and understand this. It can only help you...and you may disagree with it as it may have an impact on you.
- Goals: Has the company set goals short and long term? Do you know what they are? Knowing what they are can help you adjust or merge your work more effectively.
- Leadership: Do you respect the company's leadership? Are their values the same as yours? Understanding your leader and conforming to his/her expectations is critical in gaining trust both ways. Trust is what helps you grow.

- Objectives: Close, but not the same as goals. What are the company's objectives? You should know this as you are better able to navigate your responsibilities in a way the compliments those objectives.

- Transitions: Is the company transitioning? Are you aware of any pivoting from one direction to another? Companies that are in transition become very quiet about details during this period and usually lead strongly from the top down in order to effect direction. Be aware of any changes to the company's mission, products, advertising, etc... it can give you an up on transitioning with it.

- Changes: More obvious than transitions and are usually fraught with some unpleasant adjustments. Understanding the changes (especially if you see them coming early) will allow you to have a head start on whatever these changes may mean for you.

- Politics: Is everywhere. Understanding the company politics and how to navigate through it both with bosses and colleagues is the ultimate challenge and has rewards if played right and push back if played wrong. How do you play? Well, everyone plays different as everyone acts and reacts according to their surroundings and character. Smartly, wily, patience, and strategic is key.

- Nuances: Those details matter. The nuances of the company's performance and its employees are critical to understand. That culture that came from the nuances exist for a reason. Understanding them keeps you aware of details that others miss.

Your responsibility is to keep pace with your company... stay on point and assimilate to situations so you are not caught off guard.

74

Paralysis

Like a deer caught in the headlights... when you don't know what to do or what is expected of you, you basically freeze. Not in the sense that you do nothing, but close... as far as your career is concerned anyway. It is the sense of anxiety and the lack of fulfillment that causes this. Your habits at work become mechanical in way... routine to the point of being able to know exactly how your day will go without much planning of it.

It is unfortunate that most suffer from this paralysis. The only way to break out of it is to get serious about your own ambitions. Look, whatever most suffer means... it can also mean most are fine this way because it brings in a check every week and it provides a decent living. But, for those that are more ambitious, anxious, and unfulfilled... it is a paralysis or stalled forward progress.

If you do not know what to do to change that in your current job or your current job does not provide you with enough direction, you are paralyzed you are staying still. Your choices are to either speak up or move on. Easier said than done, true… but think about where you are or aren't and most importantly where you are going. Being comfortable feels good now, however, it will have a cause and effect later for sure.

75

Lags and Gaps

Here is an analogy... think about when you are driving (or someone else is) on the highway and the vehicle in front begins to pull further away from you leaving a gap. In most cases this is because you become zoned out so you are not keeping up your speed with the traffic in front... you begin to lag. Then what happens? Other vehicles pass you. Worse, other vehicles pass you and move in front of you. At this point you either come out of your zoned state and hit the accelerator, (so no one else gets in) or you just sit there - either because you don't care or you are not realizing what is happening. Either way... you are being jumped.

Think about your career the same way. Keep up with traffic and be aware of potentials that will pass you and move in front of you. Being aware of this will keep you in the running and spotlight when the time comes for promotions, compensation increases, important projects, etc.

76

When Times Get Tough

People get creative... Well, sometimes... it actually depends on the circumstances. In the face of competition your staff can be rallied fairly easily, provided the leadership shows confidence and has a coherent strategic plan. Also, when a cooperative environment is encouraged and instilled employees (across all hierarchal levels) become motivated... some in a way you would least expect.

On the other end, in the face of change and transition it becomes a time of fear and uncertainty. The creative nature of most become suppressed for fear of making a mistake and placing themselves in the spotlight, hence a target for change. During this period it is imperative that leaders lead in a way that calms the fears and uncertainties of employees for the good of consistency in growth.

As a leader, being aware of the tough times that exist and the effect it may be having on staff is critical. It's critical to the performance of the organization as much as it is critical to a leaders overall performance. When times get tough it is a great opportunity to see where your staff's strengths and weaknesses are, hence, affording a leader with key information as to where and how to channel current talents. From a staffs perspective it affords an opportunity to learn their own strengths and weaknesses.

Times getting tough comes in many variables to include, financial breakdown to reorganization to competitive disadvantage. Being aware and diligent in managing and providing the leadership in identifying positive aspects of tough times.

77

Predictability in Management

Just about the worst case scenario for lower productivity and waste is management and staff confused about expectations. This can come from a variety of areas to include poor or innately confused upper management, board of directors or ownership. The predictability of direction and the communication that trickles down is key to a concise, deliberate and forward moving organization.

The sheer definition of management is predictability of expectations. If that core ingredient is missing, confusion sets in. On the surface it may not be obvious, but the underlying fault is redundancy and adjustments that both cost and impact the bottom-line – almost an intangible. It may be caught by a wise manager, but would be difficult to detect by an accountant combing over monthly or quarterly reports.

There is a simple solution to this, communication. However, how can something be communicated if there is confusion from the get go in the higher ranks? It is the responsibility and obligation of those in the position of strategic goal setting to hence have those goals and expectations predictable to the very people responsible for delivering results.

From a communication stand point, this opens up a whole other statement on the issue. The predictability comes from understanding and concise communicating of intentions and the strategic plan.

78

Bad Ideas and Peripheries

Just because you think it is a good idea does not make it so. This goes to your thought, then your mouth, hence the expression, foot in your mouth.

The business world is fraught with examples of bad ideas. You can imagine the scenario of that one person delivering the idea only to have eager colleagues and/or board members jump on and... well, let's just say the trouble sets in some time down the road when everyone becomes aware that something is wrong.

The problem here does not exactly start with the bad idea. If this idea is communicated/articulated properly, perhaps an adjustment could be presented that would avoid the pitfalls of compounding errors going forward.

The adjustment(s) that may be necessary to turn a bad idea into either a good idea and/or not moving forward at all with it is the ability to see the peripheries. What does this look like from this point of view? What is vague about this? What are the parallels that can impact later down the road? These are simple questions, but nevertheless important ones when capital is considered. Producing ideas now, then pointing the finger later is too late.

Looking at the peripheries of your idea before presented or when another's idea is being considered is prudent in its fullest. It is easy to become blinded by an idea that is perceived as a money maker or career builder. Be aware of the peripheries.

79

Your Motives

Most people can hide their motives. Some cannot, this may come because they are passionate and animated about a subject.

Motives are important to us because they drive what we are attempting to claim or do.

When you are able to hide your motives, others can only speculate. Yes, that speculation can create intrigue that in turn creates suspicion that in turn creates a false impression or perception. However, by not hiding your motives you surrender tactics, weaknesses and strength. Once others know what is motivating you, they know what you are thinking. When they what you are thinking they know what motives you and you no longer have leverage. You give any tactical advantage you had away.

Going into negotiations, whether a promotion or buying a car, temper yourself and always leave your motives out.

80

The Perils of Talking too Much

There is an expression, It is better to keep your mouth shut and let people think you are stupid, then to open your mouth and confirm it. The problem is that most people do not keep their mouths shut when they should. They will involve themselves in intriguing conversations just to be a part of colleagues' clicks or to show off because they know something another does not. (By-the-way, criminals fall into this thing of talking too much – that's why they're in jail). In any event, when you talk too much others slowly piece together information about you. They form opinions based on what you are saying, not your actions. The problem with this is that the judgments being made will hinder your ability to grow in an organization. You were not promoted, you were let go, you were left out of a meeting, etc. Honestly, you will never know.

When you stay quiet, people are unsure of you. They are more apt to give you the benefit of the doubt, to trust you, to be intrigued by you.

Remember something, it is not the perception of yourself that allows you to navigate your way... it is the perception that others have of you.

81

Dismissing Others

...at your own peril. Let's forget about karma for a moment, the dismissing of others, whomever they may be, is akin to ignoring your future. Your interactions with your colleagues, subordinates, bosses, line employees, vendors, sales people, etc. creates a symbiotic (not in its direct definition) relationship that affords you a respect and perception from others that comes back to you. This is not a philosophical point, but a point in its truest form of our relationship with others. Dismissing a bad idea is different than dismissing another for their lack of status or job title.

A relationship motivated by tolerance, respect and understanding creates a more efficient environment than one of, dismissiveness or arrogance.

82

Your Assumptions Lead to Your Conclusions

The heading here should be enough to understand without much discussion or explaining.

Once you make an assumption about something, you have taken possession of it. Everything from that point sets you in a direction to reach your anticipated conclusion. The problem comes if your assumptions are wrong. Then your conclusions are wrong. Thinking clearly through the process of your assumptions... this can mean financial assumptions, capital planning assumptions, operational assumptions, anything that will lead you to a conclusion that impacts a strategic direction when expenditures, layoffs, restructuring, policy adjustments, etc. are in play can be brought to a more optimal result if the assumptions are based on more empirical information, hence, leading to a more solid conclusion.

83

Push you Off

The professional competitive nature for growth within an organization is paved with politics, performance and wily tactics.

Keeping yourself at peak is imperative. Think of it as if you're driving on a highway, but not as fast as traffic is moving. What happens? Cars are passing you in the right and left lanes, others are flashing their lights behind you, etc. You get pushed off or relegated to the right lane. It's the same with your professional growth... others that are more motivated, at peak performance, hardworking, smart, etc. will blow right passed you.

Your focus and concentration need to be evident and obvious in your performance. Understanding the culture, politics and the angles will give you an advantage in your decision making and performance. Be aware of where you are and where you are going.

84

Being Distracted

In other words… simply put, not concentrated on the right things – the things that will advance your career and/or keep you focused where you need be to remain more than relevant and performing in your position.

By not having your priorities straight and allowing yourself to float off the objectives or points that are important and relevant to your superiors' means you are distracted with less relevant things. For example, if you have an idea or a strategy on how to improve, maintain, manage a department or an aspect within it… be it a policy, performance or procedural and your superior is dropping hints or being direct that s/he disagrees or is not seeing the benefit… but, you just continue on along a certain path because you have this idea it's working - then you are distracted. You are missing the point and direction and you're focused on the wrong things… things that are not important to your boss.

As trivial as this may sound, it is a vital part of your success and your performance as a leader. You cannot be distracted by your own priorities when it differs from your bosses. It's a recipe for misunderstanding and distrust.

85

The Numbers

Look at the numbers, but don't. As important as they are, the values and decisions that come before the numbers are just as important. Many times they are intangibles. You may define a new product or policy as the value is easy to understand, but translating it into numbers does not always work. Those same intangibles are the core of what drives the numbers in an organization. They are the ideas, innovations, creativities that produce a value and benefit that customers become use to.

From an accountants perspective it becomes a bottom-line issue. Especially in the primary stages of a product or service launch. Accountants are not managers and therefore cannot see prior to the end stage when results make themselves clearer. However, even then the value and benefits of a decision can be hard to see.

The bottom line (no pun intended) is to not always be concerned with the numbers to the point that it drives all your decisions. Values are hidden in areas that the numbers can never anticipate, therefore making decisions based on something of value, either for the customer or employees brings something much more important.

86

Keeping Them Down

This refers to your employees.

A sure way to lose talent... and in the process erode your bottom-line is to suppress the abilities of your employees. There are a number of ways this happens.

- Micro-Managing: No one would dispute that the ownership or higher management has the right and prerogative in setting the direction of an organization. However, there are times when this becomes more of an interference than beneficial to an organizations progress. Micro-management undermines and usurps the talent hired to make things run efficiently.
- Not Identifying: The inability or carelessness of not identifying what specific talents your employees have is detrimental in a number of ways. 1) Productivity and wages. 2) Inefficiency of resource allocation. 3) Moral killer.

- Kills... Drive, Moral, creativity, innovation, potential and everything else that comes with suppressing or keeping them (talent) down.

It is very much a description of wasting resources on many levels. Leaders are required to know the details of their employee's talents and where they would best be positioned/ utilized to optimal value. It is just as important that the employee is where they want to be, hence having them enjoy what they do... that in-turn brings productivity, innovation, creativity, etc.

Let's not over think this. The idea is not to create a playground for talent, but to create an environment that is conducive to productivity. It's a win-win.

87

Hypothesis

You should have one.

All this means is that you have a testable prediction about what you expect to happen. In this case, your career or life goals/expectations. This is not the specific definition of course, but close enough for our purpose here.

In other words... you should be constantly balancing where you are or where you're going or where you want to be – in 3 years, 5 years, 10 years, etc. Assessing your position and creating a hypothesis for yourself is prudent as it keeps you aware and moving before boredom or stagnation set in.

The worse thing that can happen to you is for you to wake up one day and say, "How the heck did I get here." Or worse, "How the heck did I not get there."

Daily Business Thoughts
by John Canavan

Think your growth...

Hey! Don't cut others down or throw them under the bus to justify your relevance and/or position. Stand on your own, and focus yourself.

Do the work that you know and love...this way fulfillment equals productivity...whereas the opposite equals tolerance and meritocracy.

As with everything...hope and faith is not enough to advance your career. Planning at a minimum gives you an idea to work with.

Try and see things from a distance...a perspective away from within gives you the context and oppty. of a broader solution and direction.

Remember, others are not actively working against you. They are simply looking out for themselves. It's up to you to manage the circumstances

---

Choosing and surrounding yourself with the right people, is the difference between success and stagnation.

Your relevance as a leader is predicated on your proactive decisions and judgments, not your attempts to get yourself noticed with noise.

United we stand, divided we fall. Not empty words. During organizational change and transition, those words are more important than ever.

Big decisions come more than once in a while...most of the time unexpected. Some of these decisions are literally life changers. Know which.

Complacent yes men/people go nowhere fast. Why? A lack of ideas and autonomy. There's another name for it...

Have you ever heard others say, "don't judge."? Well, they judge most. We all judge all the time, work and play. Make yourself less visible.

Technology...it's all over the place, and it's not stopping - on the contrary. However, it's not what makes things go round. It's people.

What stands you apart from the rest of the herd? Remember, majorities are always led, they never lead. Your individuality will forward you.

There's always a choice...when you reach that point, you should know, and quickly assimilate your choice(s) to attempt the most prudent one.

The boredom in managing to just manage...challenge the mundane and usual...the benefits may not always come, but at least you allow a chance.

To wit...navigate your career as though others want the same positions you do - because they do. The challenges you endure are for a reason.

Although the word, "arrogance" comes from a less derogatory meaning in Latin, nevertheless, in English it is an attribute of poor manners.

Water may just have it right...path of least and easiest resistance. If you are over stressed maybe you are in the wrong job or life path.

Paying attention...it makes all the difference in the world to your understanding and results. It's a form of awareness. Both Prof. / Pers.

When not prepared...fear, anxiety, anxiousness, confusion, insecurity, heaviness, etc. sets in. Not good. Prepare and define the opposites.

Careful not to attack another's motives in negotiation or debate. Attack the facts, attack the context. Otherwise your position faults.

Your focus...is what determines your progress. Btwn multitasking and ADHD we're all over the place. Put attention...focus smartly on things.

Choice...many excuses arise as to why you can't do what you really want. Barriers are placed by you alone. Choose without fear and it moves.

Remember... love what you do for work and you will never work a day in your life.

You have to know who you are first in order to know what you want. Know what you want and navigate in that direction. Don't...then float on.

Let's define a managers/a leaders responsibility as many forget. Create clear and predictable policies, procedures, strategies...

Many people search for a problem where none exists. It helps them feel/seem relevant. Real problem solving is doing, not creating new ones.

If you want to lead tomorrow, you must think about tomorrow. Navigate your moves today, so they echo through tomorrow.

There is a big difference btwn what is expected of you and what you expect of yourself.

Downtime - meaning a scenery change...is underrated and should be a mandatory part of your leadership...both for you and the ones you lead.

Inattention will defeat you every time. It's the course that will place your future in your past before you get there.

Power...there is a lot said about it. A leader in any capacity has it. Watch them...their character...are they fair, just, aware, strategic?

Think of a shark...it's always moving - always. Water must flow through its gills or it dies. Now, think of yourself in the same way. Move.

Your equilibrium...it defines your comfort zone in the context of your work environment. When off, there is disorientation. Know it, fix it.

Create the right culture in your organization and watch its productivity soar. It is the responsibility of the leader to do so.

A mix btwn Generation Baby Boomers and Generation Y is the right balance in terms of workplace productivity, values, culture. Understand it.

Time...something that is relentless. It passes whether you are paying attention or not. Be aware of it and use it to your advantage.

Thoughts of abundance vs. thoughts of scarcity. It's not the difference btwn positive and negative thinking...it's knowing there is plenty.

Your experience, hence knowledge that has brought you to a position of leadership demands that you guide/teach subordinates with tolerance.

Thou shalt not bear false witness. It is gossip at its core and creates intrigue for no reason except to keep the mouth busy. Don't do it.

As a leader...when you practice empathy, you understand others better, you understand the value of their input, hence providing clarity.

Networking is good...friends are good...but rely on yourself for when the time comes you know you can rely on someone you trust.

You need to see the angles...all the time. That's strategic thinking. It gives you leverage and advantage in decision making.

Your optimism works only as well as the efforts you apply to what you are optimistic about.

Adversity comes in many forms...most times when least expected. Leaders are able to handle this with poise, grace, and effectiveness.

Embrace change... When you do, you are part of the solution. When you don't you are part of the reason for the change.

What's your equilibrium? Where are you most comfortable? If your sense is off your performance is off.

Shakespeare... not the first name you would think about for business savvy... however, read a little and learn a little.

Leadership 101...create a consistent and predictable strategy and direction so your subordinates understand and expectations are realized.

Leadership driven by ego vs leadership driven by confidence... ego is all about me, I'm in charge, look at me. Confidence looks outward.

The threshold to change comes from the strategic details put in place in early planning. Skip this part and it's akin to winging it.

When politics are afoot in the workplace, relationships break down. When relationships breakdown gaps in efficiencies arise.

You can complain, but really... who's listening? Buckle down, do your work.

Stay at peak, aware of your surroundings. A lot happens that may get by you if you're not paying attention.

A fractured hierarchy is a chaotic hierarchy, or worse... confused and unfocused... For a business it is inefficient and costly. Not good.

Without empathy for a colleague, subordinate, leader, or for the situation of another...where schadenfreude exists only selfishness exists.

Leadership is the act of making decisions and confronting issues with unwavering confidence, deliberate direction, honesty and humility.

Kiss asses always think they are secure in their positions...they may be for a little while, but have you ever met a successful kiss ass?

A sure way to drive down innovation, creativity, performance, etc is to drive down confidence in your staff.

Wow! Look at all that stuff you did and accomplished...that's great! Not many people care what you did. Take it and go forward...

Yes...it is how you perceive yourself that drives your confidence, but it is how others perceive you that will drive your success.

What is your purpose? To get up in the morning to work at something you don't enjoy? That's not a purpose, it's stupid. Love what you do.

Don't be afraid.

You've heard the saying, "It's the process." Well, it is. Without it nothing happens. There's a process to success.

If you are irritable of where you are, procrastinating on what to do or floating through your days...time to check your thinking.

Living in the present is all nice and all...but not planning or having a strategy/direction for the future only keeps you in neutral.

Work 12-14 hours a day...sometimes weekends? Well, if you're enjoying what you do or the company is yours - good, if not, yikes! Not good

Find and settle into a job that you do not hold passion for and find yourself in the abyss of mundane, routine, unfulfilled and no growth.

Teams... when is this fad in the corporate world going to be over? Thanks team, good work team, see you tomorrow team...it's childish.

A leaders constraint of their managers is a recipe for failed objectives. Un-constrain them and you succeed.

The office place is full of politics, full of unfairness and fairness and choices - some big. Think long term before you make choices.

A leaders goals must be clear or it is his/her fault in failure. If clear, then managers are at fault - blaming staff is an excuse.

The days of managing through command and control...can only have long term drawbacks. With a new demographic comes new thinking. Careful.

We communicate based on our experience, disposition and perception. Always room for misunderstanding. Don't just hear. Look and listen well.

If you have a doubt...pause. This means you are questioning something. It is different than a gut feeling. When in doubt, pause, assess...

We all fail...the trick is to tower your failures over others successes.

Business is serious business. Your employers (they are the people that are paying you money) expect you to understand this.

How quickly your fortunes can turn...for better or for worse. Always be prepared mentally for both...strong, but humble is key.

Employees are motivated by 3 things... Feeling valued, having trust, and understanding the direction/objectives/goals.

Exaggerations and embellishments...the tools for those that lack relevance.

The essence of inefficiency is... procrastination and carelessness.

Loyalty...don't look for it, don't wait for it, don't expect it... move forward with your own purpose.

There is a difference between looking busy and being busy. And most people can tell when you're trying to look busy... and relevant.

As circumstances are, not everything goes smooth. The creators and innovators are easily criticized. Must be nice to be a follower.

Concentrate on the details of the details and watch everything slow down.

Always be leery of someone who says to you, "Hey, it's just business." That's the age old excuse for, "I'm ready to screw you."

Although the office environment does not have to be, "Can we all just get along?" It does not have to be Cut and Slash either.

It is through clarity that things get done. Don't communicate and watch your strategy disintegrate.

Mentally prepare yourself, visualize before you enter meetings or situations... By doing so your mind will be in the right place.

People don't change. Have you heard that before? Well, it's not true. A saying created by those that can't. People change all the time.

When you are organized, this translates into higher efficiency. When your area of responsibility is un-kept, so then is productivity.

Try not to have a hard view of the world, of people...your perception begets the same of you and makes work and play not pleasant.

Yes...you will make mistakes. But, there is a cure. Do nothing.

Let's face it...many meetings are useless. Attendees are either there to score points, socialize or just glad to be invited. Control agenda!

You go to a place on vacation and say, I'd like to live here. Well, the world is populated with nay sayers...it can be done. Don't be afraid.

Let us get this straight...your job does not owe you anything, so if there is no edifying then you need to think about your situation.

Careful with those gut feelings...although sometimes useful, many times they are based on your fears and insecurities. Use logic more.

Always be aware of the happenings in your life...be able to identify events and situations that will afford you positive opportunities...

To ignore or not ignore those petty rumors and talkiness around you. Engaging in gossip disengages you from your serious goals.

Awareness...it's what separates us from everything else. Be aware of your surroundings - adjust as you go, remember, look around, prepare...

Anyone's life can become upended by circumstances unforeseen...or even foreseen. However, your preparation of such is imperative. Plan now.

You don't feel appreciated? Get over it and move on. Your fulfillment is yours...there are few that will allow you credit. Keep moving...

Performance above all...otherwise what is the purpose. Your employees perform when they know where they stand. Transparency... Talk to them.

Surrounding yourself with smart/good people is just part of it...your responsibility is leading them and giving them the tools...

Don't over analyze or over think so much... Remember that the simplest explanation is usually the right one.

Whatever business you are in...whether you manage a department, manage the business or own the business...create and innovate - or else...

Lament on the past and stay stuck there. Look over the horizon...and you're going places.

Know what you are thinking... control your thoughts so you are consistent in your interactions with others. No one likes a chameleon.

Know that you did not get where you are on your own... someone someplace had something to do with how you got there. It's called being humble.

At work you have interests, not friends.

Idea fluidity... keep your mind moving and ideas flowing or cede your spot to others that do.

Talking problems leads to nowhereville. Talking solutions leads to somewhereville. Having the problem is okay, staying stuck on it is not.

Important are you? The cemeteries are filled with indispensable people. Put things in perspective.

Employees work best, are creative, are innovative, remain loyal, etc. when they are valued. Sap that value and watch the reverse.

When stressed and overwhelmed at work...slow your thinking, departmentalize, assess, prioritize. Know good stress from pressure stress.

Your attitude is what propels you forward or holds you back. Understand your mindset and disposition.

Business 101... Never criticize your predecessor or successor.

As boss your responsibility is to encourage and inspire your staff. Ignoring, criticizing, isolating, dismissing, begets the same.

The grass is always greener on the other side...then, the grass is always greener on the other side...get it? Water the grass where you are.

The amount of time you spend on nonsense thoughts of fear, turf protection, motives of others...is time wasted and growth restrictive.

As a leader... Set others up for success, not failure. It's your duty.

When you over think and over analyze...your mind fabricates, exaggerates, creates what's not there. Don't let your thoughts runaway. Think.

Get your mind in the right place...it is how you perceive your situation. If you perceive work as being, not good - then it's not. Get it?

It's better to stay quiet and let people think you don't know, then to open your mouth and confirm it. Know before you speak.

Your Strategic Focus should be looking beyond the numbers.

Sunday anxiety...if you get it then something is wrong with what you're doing Mondays. Are you happy in your job?

When you throw a colleague or whoever under the bus because it makes you look good...trust me, you don't look good. You look ineffectual.

Want a text book example of business inefficiency? The congressional debt deal. A deal that's not a deal at all and what it took to get there.

Decisions through/with a committee spreads the risk and gets all on board. Go solo in a power grab and watch the inefficiencies grow.

Are you in charge? Then act like it.

In college? Having fun? You better start thinking about what you want to do when you're out. That strategy begins now... not then.

Where are you in your career? Are you satisfied, fulfilled? Don't get stuck. Always look ahead...Your professional growth needs attention.

You have a plan? Going well is it? Well, make sure you're prepared for that "stuff happens" thing that derails your plan. Prepare to adjust.

Be aloof in your disciplines while at the office. In other words...you know what to do - concentrate on your work and don't kiss ass.

Take it easy on the e-mails. Not all of us have as much time to read it as you did writing it. Be concise and to the point.

Go ahead...take risks - it invites success.

When you gossip at work - creating intrigue, it means you're not working. Get the fantasies out of your head...it's annoying to others.

Engage your employees with a sense of purpose. Challenging employees through engagement and positive reinforcement... not by barking orders.

What are you doing inviting or accepting anyone/everyone to connect with you on Linkedin? Just to get your number up? Stop...be selective.

As a leader, you are only as successful as the quality of resources you contribute to your subordinates.

About the Author

John Canavan was born, raised and educated in New York City. He is an avid studier of Business Philosophy and Strategic Planning. He currently works in the hospitality/tourism trade, had owned and operated businesses in the United States and abroad and has consulted for small businesses through FocuStrategy concentrating on Strategic Planning and Turnaround.

John also advises, coaches and mentors business leaders, managers and college students in their efforts to increase their productivity and navigate their career challenges and direction. You can follow John on twitter – johncanavan@ focustrategy

Books:
FocuStrategy: Navigating Your Professional Growth (Vol. I)

Online:
www.focustrategy.com
focustrategy@twitter
focustrategy@tumblr
Facebook–focustrategy

Other interests include:
www.InterimGM.com